SIMPLE STEPS FOR EVERY HOLIDAY

An Easy Plan for

More Joyful, Less Stressful

Celebrations All Year Long

SIMPLE STEPS
FOR EVERY HOLIDAY

An Easy Plan for

More Joyful, Less Stressful

Celebrations All Year Long

Health ✦ Fitness ✦ Home ✦ Family ✦ Self

Lisa Lelas

Linda McClintock

Beverly Zingarella

NEW AMERICAN LIBRARY

New American Library
Published by New American Library, a division of
Penguin Group (USA) Inc., 375 Hudson Street,
New York, New York 10014, USA
Penguin Group (Canada), 10 Alcorn Avenue, Toronto,
Ontario, Canada M4V 3B2 (a division of Pearson Penguin Canada Inc.)
Penguin Books Ltd., 80 Strand, London WC2R 0RL, England
Penguin Ireland, 25 St Stephen's Green, Dublin 2, Ireland
(a division of Penguin Books Ltd.)
Penguin Group (Australia), 250 Camberwell Road, Camberwell,
Victoria 3124, Australia (a division of Pearson Australia Group Pty. Ltd.)
Penguin Books India Pvt. Ltd., 11 Community Centre, Panchsheel Park,
New Delhi - 110 017, India
Penguin Books (NZ), Cnr Airborne and Rosedale Roads,
Albany, Auckland, New Zealand (a division of Pearson New Zealand Ltd.)
Penguin Books (South Africa) (Pty.) Ltd., 24 Sturdee Avenue,
Rosebank, Johannesburg 2196, South Africa

Penguin Books Ltd., Registered Offices:
80 Strand, London WC2R 0RL, England

First Printing, November 2004
10   9   8   7   6   5   4   3   2   1

(NAL) REGISTERED TRADEMARK—MARCA REGISTRADA

LIBRARY OF CONGRESS CATALOGING-IN-PUBLICATION DATA:

Lelas, Lisa.
Simple steps for every holiday : an easy plan for more joyful, less
stressful celebrations all year long : health, fitness, home, family, self /
Lisa Lelas, Linda McClintock, and Beverly Zingarella.
p.   cm.
Includes bibliographical references.
ISBN 0-451-21360-2 (trade pbk.)
1.   Home economics.   I. McClintock, Linda.   II. Zingarella, Beverly.   III. Title.
TX147.L44 2004
640—dc22
2004012006

Set in Filosofia
Designed by Jennifer Ann Daddio

Printed in the United States of America

With love and sweet admiration, this book is
dedicated to my parents, Hans and Lotte Weiss,
and my grandparents for providing me with a
childhood so rich with warm European holiday
traditions; to my husband, John, and to my beautiful
girls, Lindsay and Lexy, with whom each holiday
is magnified through their eyes, and who prove
that every day is a worthwhile celebration!
—LL

✦

I dedicate this book to my grandparents, Katharine
and Michael Weiss and Elisabeth and Hans Hackner,
for passing down such treasured cultural holiday
traditions from their country. To my parents Hans
and Lotte Weiss and to my in-laws, Caroline and
Russell McClintock, for all of their wonderful
family stories and history To my husband,
Duncan, and son, Michael, who make
celebrating every tradition so priceless!
—LM

✦

With much love I dedicate this book to my parents,
George and Dolores Adamson, and my mother-in-law,
Eleanor Zingarella, for the many gifts of holiday
traditions they have shared with me. And to my
husband, Tom, and children, Alicia, Matthew,
and Lucian, for continuing to share the old
and establish new holiday traditions.
—BZ

Acknowledgments

Writing this book would not have been possible without the natural love for the holidays that we each possess, a love that was fostered by the joyous traditions passed down by our parents, our grandparents, and our ancestors before them. We would like to thank each and every member of our extended families (including aunts, uncles, cousins, in-laws, nieces, and nephews) with whom we have shared so many holidays. We have enjoyed igniting that flame of holiday joy together over the years!

These three ladies would like to also send hugs and kisses to the other three ladies of *Simple Steps*. . . . Thank you to Carol Mann, our supportive agent, who saw the *Simple Steps* series long before we did, to our wonderful editor, Claire Zion, for embracing us with her encouragement, and to Jessica Papin for all her creative vision.

And a big bundle of thanks to all of our *Simple Steps* readers and fans throughout the world. We love hearing from you (and promise that we really read each and every letter/e-mail sent). It is because of all of your support and kind words that we continue our *Simple Steps* journey into the magical world of holiday celebrations!

—*Lisa, Linda, and Beverly*

Contents

A Time to Celebrate!

The Simple Steps *Story*

When we took the very first steps toward transforming our lives by designing a personal lifestyle program, we had no idea what lay ahead! What an amazing journey it has been since the publication of our first book, *Simple Steps: 10 Weeks to Getting Control of Your Life*. Not only have we all succeeded in getting control of our own lives again, but it seems that our stories of encouragement have touched the lives of many others.

Throughout this journey, we have been fortunate to meet or correspond with devoted "Simple Steppers" from around the world, all of whom remind us of just how connected we all are, and how small the universe becomes when we actually reach out to touch it.

Simple Steps has enriched our lives with so many new

adventures. From our first appearances on *Oprah,* to book signings, to an appearance on *Today*, to a lifestyle summer challenge series on Comcast cable, to a regular radio feature, to wellness workshops for hospitals and lectures across the country—we can hardly believe how responsive people are, or how powerful a "simple" message can be.

We have learned and grown from our experiences: All three of us believe we have indeed become better wives and mothers as a result of creating and following *Simple Steps*, but perhaps most significantly, we feel we have enriched our *selves*. In taking one simple step after another, we've found the joy and peace in our hearts that come with a renewed sense of balance and pride.

The three of us have blossomed into sturdy sunflowers, reaching new heights every day. Now, when we gaze into the looking glass, we not only see three busy entrepreneurs who have found their passion in life, but we also see *ourselves* again . . . this time happier and more fulfilled, with no missing pieces.

Come with us now and share our joy as we continue on the *Simple Steps* journey, this time on an exploration of the holidays and festivals that so enhance our lives. We'd love to hear from you too. Share with us, if you will, your own family celebrations and holiday tips for easier living! Log onto www.SimpleStepsProgram.com, or write Simple Steps for Every Holiday, P.O. Box 128, Guilford, CT 06437.

Cheers to celebrating together!

—*Lisa, Linda, and Beverly*

Authors' Updates

Lisa's Story: I am truly grateful to be able to live and breathe my dream life! Although I tend to wear several "life hats" and admit that it's sometimes a challenge to maintain a sense of balance, I am satisfied that I am keeping busy with only those things that I love: my children and family, and a career devoted to inspiring others.

I became a life coach from my own need to find balance, and I am now a professional organizer and an active member of the National Association of Professional Organizers. Currently I serve on the executive board of its Connecticut chapter. I write weekly and monthly columns ("Life Styling" and "Office Styling") for several newspapers and magazines, and tour the country giving motivational lectures on the subjects of organizing, decluttering, and creating a life plan.

In order to carve out time to write each day, book lectures each week, help organize and coach others, stay involved with many social and civic organizations (I am PTO president!), *plus* spend time with my husband and two daughters—each of whom has her own activities—time management is essential for me. I suspect it is essential for everyone.

I have come to the realization that organizing and inspiring others to organize their lives and follow their dreams really is my *passion*. Whether pulling together a workable system for a client's office files or kitchen pantry, setting up an efficient schedule for my own family, or designing a road map for attaining future goals, I know in my heart that I am doing what I love, and in doing so, I am serving as a positive role model for my daughters.

Readers are always welcome to e-mail me at SimpleSteps Program@hotmail.com. *Lisa's favorite holiday celebrations:* The entire twenty-five-day Christmas season, New Year's Day, July Fourth picnics at the beach, and Lindsay's and Lexy's birthdays each February and October!

Linda's Story: Time sure flies when you're having fun! It seems like just moments ago that my son was a toddler and I was beginning the *Simple Steps* journey. I am fortunate to be able to stay home to raise my son, who is now about to turn five years old. And I feel I am fortunate to be able to embark on new creative endeavors on a regular basis.

Simple Steps has given me a chance to meet many wonderful people from all over the world—some of whom have become good friends. Moreover, it has helped me find the courage to follow my heart; I've signed up at the New England School of Feng Shui to study to be a feng shui consultant. I have long been intrigued by this ancient Chinese art of cultivating positive energy and better living. Now I'm enjoying every minute that I spend learning, creating, and being with such positive people.

With classes to attend, homework to complete, *Simple Steps* workshops to do, and a very active son who needs my attention, free time is a precious commodity for me. Still, I know that in keeping busy, I am sending Michael a good message: Follow your heart and carve out the time needed to do those things you were meant to do. I also teach Sunday school at our church and am a member of the National Association of Professional Organizers.

Readers can e-mail me at SimpleStepsProgram@ hotmail.com. I would love to hear from you.

Linda's favorite holiday celebrations: All holidays are special when I'm spending them with my family, but I particularly love watching my son's face on Christmas morning after he sneaks downstairs; celebrating special birthdays and baking equally special birthday cakes; and sharing the magic of Halloween with my son!

Beverly's Story: My goodness, my life has changed! When my *Simple Steps* journey began I remember how exciting it was to share our lifestyle program with others. At first, I was nervous and hesitant about public speaking. To my surprise, the nervousness faded immediately after I led my very first lifestyle-makeover group. Teaching and encouraging others to work toward life goals filled me with a wonderful sense of empowerment.

I am grateful for the opportunities coauthoring *Simple Steps* has afforded me. Along with teaching others, I continue to learn so much about myself. In the years to come I would love to continue to motivate and inspire others to live their best life and set priorities. I strongly believe in the principles of *Simple Steps* . . . encouraging others to stop "rushing" through life and set goals. I love to offer advice and inspire others, both through answering e-mails and lecturing, as well as facilitating *Simple Steps* group programs.

Since I have a husband, three children, two dogs, and a

cat, balance is of utmost importance. My family is my priority, and I pride myself on the fact that my days are filled doing exactly what I love . . . nurturing and guiding my children as well as being a positive role model. I am active in my children's schools and our church.

Beverly's favorite holiday celebrations: Easter has always been my very favorite holiday celebration. I love everything Easter represents—faith, hope, and renewal. And, of course, Alicia's, Matthew's, and Lucian's birthdays are three of the most celebrated days in our home.

Some Notes on Using This Book

Although we've organized this book month by month, according to holidays, feel free to incorporate these simple steps when and how you see fit. We begin spring cleaning in March, but you may prefer to wait until April.

We know that at the holidays, one of the hardest things is coming up with *what* to cook. How many times have we all wandered aimlessly through grocery store aisles, wasting time and energy and emerging with an astonishingly expensive assortment of food that somehow does not add up to a meal? In the Health sections, we furnish readers with handy menu suggestions. For specific recipes, you can rely on your own favorite cookbooks, go to the SimpleStepsprogram.com Web site, or check out one of the following of our favorite resources: *Cooking Thin with Chef Kathleen* by Kathleen Daelemans; *Cooking Light Annual Recipes* and *Cooking Light* magazine; *The Healthy Kitchen* by Andrew Weil, M.D., and Rosie Daley; *Canyon Ranch Cooking: Bringing the Spa Home* by Jeanne Jones; *New Dieter's Cookbook* by Better Homes and Gardens; *Cooking the Whole Foods Way* by Christina Pirello; *The Golden Door Cookbook* by Michel Stroot; *In the Kitchen with Rosie: Oprah's Favorite Recipes* by Rosie Daley; any of the Weight Watchers cookbooks; www.foodtv.com; and the Better Homes and Gardens Web site at www.bhg.com.

We also know that when you're a holiday hostess, planning for the right amount of food to serve can be stressful. Here's a simple guide to help you. Simply multiply the individual serving size by the number of guests you anticipate coming:

Appetizers: 5–6 pieces (approx ½ cup)
Dips: 1 tbsp.
Meat/Poultry/Fish: 4–5 oz.
Condiments: 2 tsp.
Side Dishes: ½ cup
Ice Cream: ½ cup

Finally, bear in mind that the suggestions in the Fitness section are not meant to substitute for a physician-supervised exercise program, and that before embarking on any kind of fitness regimen, you should first check in with your doctor. But as a general rule of thumb, when strength training, start with as heavy a weight as you can comfortably manage, even if it's only two pounds. The weight should be challenging, but you should be able to complete a full set without compromising correct form.

Enjoy!

January

New Year's Day

Quite possibly the oldest of holidays, the birth of the
new year has been celebrated since ancient times,
when the Babylonians first welcomed the spring
four thousand years ago. The date was shifted to the
first of January when Julius Caesar instituted the
eponymous Julian calendar, and remained
unchanged under the Gregorian calendar. It has
become a day to celebrate new beginnings!

Health

- As we all know, January 1 is *the* day to resolve to stick to a
  healthier lifestyle! But you cannot change bad eating
  habits until you analyze exactly what they are. So tip
  number one for the New Year is: Start a food journal.
  Start a fresh journal, and leave it out on your kitchen
  counter so you can log in *everything* you eat and drink.
  Yes, that includes the New Year's Day mimosa!
- Throw away your membership card to the clean-plate
  club. Resolve to leave something on your plate at every
  meal . . . even dessert. Almost 30 percent of Americans
  admit that when they eat out, they always finish their
  meal, regardless of the size of the portion.

- Draw up a contract with yourself, listing your New Year's resolutions, but don't choose more than five; set goals that you can realistically achieve. Sign it and hang it where you will be reminded of it often.

FUN FACTS: NEW YEAR'S DAY

Thirty-seven percent of Americans who make New Year's resolutions say they are "very confident" they will stick to their resolutions throughout the entire year. Eighty-two percent resolve to lose weight but do not accomplish their goal by June.

- Set up a reward plan if weight loss is a goal this year. For every ten pounds you lose, treat yourself to a movie matinee with friends, or buy a new book or a new outfit—after all, every ten pounds is a new dress size!
- Surround yourself with motivators. Prominently display a size-too-small skirt, post a picture of a strong, fit woman, or perhaps put a photo of yourself at a better weight on your refrigerator. Whenever you feel hungry, close your eyes and breathe. Imagine how you will look after you get fit.
- Give your pantry and fridge a diet-friendly makeover. Do this *before* you meet friends for holiday celebrating. Have a big garbage bag handy and toss anything you know you should not be eating. Replace sugar cereal with

high-fiber cereal and white breads with whole-grain bread. If your freezer and fridge are filled with high-fat foods, such as whole milk, deli meats, and prepackaged foods that are made with hydrogenated oils, you know you need to change your choices. "People with diets high in saturated fat are more prone to storing flab around their vital organs than those who eat a diet rich in unsaturated fats. This kind of fat, called visceral fat, puts them at greater risk for developing heart disease and diabetes," says Kerry J. Stewart, Ed.D, director of clinical exercise physiology at Johns Hopkins University School of Medicine. Saturated fats should comprise no more than 10 percent of your daily caloric intake.

- Eat with the lights turned on in the kitchen or dining room. It's been proven that the brighter the lights, the less likely you are to overeat—restaurants have dim lighting for a reason!

- Too much partying last night? Here's a secret to keep morning-after bloating at bay: Snack on celery stalks. Celery contains a compound that flushes excess fluid from your system, and unlike over-the-counter diuretics, celery won't disrupt your body's balance of sodium and potassium, which can lead to dehydration.

- Relieve postparty stomach upset with herb tea. According to New York herbalist Cheryl J.Questell, always keep the following tummy-soothing teas in your pantry: slippery elm, red raspberry, chickweed, red clover, and mint tea. To help digest a meal that's not settling, sprinkle a little nutmeg on your dessert. If you're suffering from a champagne hangover, borage or thyme tea will help you. Fennel tea in your bathwater will help release the toxins in your body.

· Don't feel like cooking up and serving a full-fare breakfast, lunch, or dinner? Arrange your holiday get-together as an "open house," and invite guests to stop in anytime (be sure to give time parameters on your invitations) for an array of appetizers and dessert that can be left out for several hours.

READER TO READER

I enjoy my annual tradition of hosting a New Year's Day open house. I tell my friends they can visit anytime between ten and three P.M., no RSVP needed. I provide the fixings for mimosas, an egg dish, and some sweet treats. Guests contribute whatever they wish . . . appetizers, music, wine, or just their company. This gets the New Year off to a loving and magical start for all of us.

—Elaine B., Norwich, Connecticut

· Consider ordering pizza for a no-fuss party meal today. Pizza can be healthy, provided you skip nitrate- and sodium-loaded meat toppings and go heavy on the veggies. Pizza sauce is rich in tomatoes (a good source of lycopene, an antioxidant that may protect against certain cancers and heart disease), and cheese is a great source of calcium (which helps build healthy bones and teeth). Blot your slice with a napkin and you can remove up to 100 calories of oil!

· Since you don't want to spend New Year's Eve in the kitchen, prepare the dishes for your New Year's brunch well ahead of time. For example, instead of having to peel, cook, and mash potatoes, consider making a healthier, freezer-friendly version out of cauliflower that you can whip up days before your party.

· If you're inclined to cook for your guests, start with a fresh vegetable soup as your first course; like carrot, tomato, or butternut squash ('tis the season for comfort food, after all!). Try replacing the cream with an evaporated skim milk or fat-free buttermilk. By beginning your meal with a healthy bowl of soup, you'll be less likely to overeat during the main course. Soup eaters save at least 100 calories at mealtime and can lose up to ten pounds a year.

SIMPLE SUGGESTIONS FOR CELEBRATORY MEALS

Often, the foods we eat at New Year's are thought to bring us good luck. In many countries, food shaped in a ring symbolizes "coming full circle," as we complete a full year and start a new one. Examples include doughnuts, Bundt cakes, and bread baked in a ring. In the Southern United States, hopping John is traditional New Year's fare, made with black-eyed peas and ham. The idea behind the simple dish is to "eat poorly one day and eat rich the rest of the year." Cabbage

represents paper money, and eating it on New Year's is believed to guarantee a prosperous year, while in many Asian
cultures, rice is a lucky food and is eaten on New Year's Day.

Fitness

- Did you know that, every year, the number one–rated
  New Year's resolution is to exercise? Don't be so quick
  to spend your money on a pricey membership. Gyms are
  the most crowded during the month of January with
  well-intentioned resolution makers. Better to make
  fitness a part of your daily routine at home by adding
  thirty minutes a day of walking and some free-weight
  exercise. *Then* join the gym in February, once you've
  proven your resolve.
- Make a wellness date today. Instead of socializing with
  your girlfriends over drinks, meet for a winter hike, go
  ice skating, help shovel each other's driveways, or head
  to the local Y for a swim (most will sell day passes if
  you're not a member). Creating a team can provide the
  encouragement you need, especially this month, when
  you're working toward establishing a commitment
  toward your fitness goals.
- Add a fitness component to your food journal. Begin by
  writing down your fitness goals; aim for doing some
  kind of physical activity five days per week. Thereafter,
  use the journal to record your progress while working
  out. Record your cardio activity (type and duration) and

strength training sets (reps and intensity) and how you feel after each workout.

- If you're considering joining a gym next month, take time in January to call all of the gyms in your area and set up appointments to tour and try each facility. You'll have a better notion of which you want to join, and will get a few free workouts to boot.

FITNESS FOCUS: WALKING

Many people find walking to be the best way to start a fitness program. Moreover, walking eases back pain, slims your waist, is easy on your joints, strengthens your bones, shapes your legs and butt, lowers blood pressure, and reduces your risk of heart disease and diabetes. It requires no equipment, can be done anywhere, and allows time with family and friends. A study of depressed people ages fifty to seventy-seven found that when they took a brisk thirty-minute walk at least three days a week they had improved moods and sharper memories.

- Buy a pedometer this week and wear it. Walking ten thousand steps per day burns as many calories as working out for thirty minutes. And if you have a specific measured goal, you'll be less likely to end your walk too soon.
- Chances are, your inaugural walk of the New Year will take place in wintry weather. Keep in mind the following cold-weather dos and don'ts from the Mayo Clinic. Be sure to dress appropriately: Wear lightweight, breathable layers, even on your hands and feet, shoes

with good traction to handle slippery conditions, a hat to combat heat loss, as well as scarf or face mask to warm your breath. Be sure to warm up slowly—avoid going outside when you're already sweating. Drink plenty of water—you may not feel as thirsty as when it's hot out,

---

CHITCHAT

As a writer, I have found the best cure for the dreaded "writer's block" is to leave my desk and get outside for a walk. I picked up a wonderful tip from several members of my local writers group, and before I set out, I tuck a pencil and a blank index card in my pocket, folded in half and sticking out slightly for easy retrieval. As creative ideas pop into my head, I immediately jot them down on the card. Without getting too technical, I have done some research on "walking-induced creativity" and it appears it's a real, scientifically observable phenomenon. Apparently, after the first five minutes that you spend listening to the repetitive sounds of walking, the left side of your brain (the "practical half" responsible for reasoning) gets "bored" and naturally kicks the right (creative) side into gear. So, if you have problems to be solved, papers to be written, or just want to get in touch with your creativity . . . start walking!

—Lisa Lelas

but you need to stay hydrated. Finally, be sure the wind
is at your back on the return leg of your walk.

HOME Décor

- Stow away the December decorations the first week of
  the New Year (see tips below). In your décor for January,
  celebrate a respite from holiday clutter. Empty surfaces,
  open curtains, let in light with the New Year.
- Can't *quite* go cold turkey on home decoration? Today,
  replace your evergreen holiday wreath with a bright
  midwinter model. Think bright dried or silk flowers,
  eucalyptus, pinecones, and juniper berries. Small white
  dried flowers are particularly striking.
- Treat yourself to a New Year's bouquet of fresh flowers.
  Place them on your kitchen table so you can see them all
  day long.
- If you are hosting a New Year's brunch for friends, make
  "New Year, New You" an official theme: place food
  platters on trivets made from stacks of diet and exercise
  books. A festive yet inspirational new look for your
  table!

HOMEkeeping and Organization

- Pack up your Christmas decorations as early in the
  month as you can. And when you do, consider redoing
  your old holiday storage system. Ditch the battered,

oddly sized cardboard boxes and replace them with
inexpensive plastic storage bins (several smaller ones
are actually easier to use than one too-big-to-carry bin).
Label the bins, or better yet, buy clear ones. Toss any
decorations that you no longer use.

- Recycle your Christmas tree. Call your town and inquire
whether there is local tree pickup or see if you can
donate it. Many scout troops collect trees after the
holidays and chip and mulch them for use in flower beds
in spring.

- Before you toss or put away holiday cards that you've
received, be sure to update your holiday-card address
list. Don't stow it away with other seasonal items, but
instead keep the list somewhere handy so you can add
and refer to it all year long.

- Make use of that old box of nails in your husband's
toolbox. By hammering a few big nails (halfway only!)
into the studs of your basement or attic storage, you've
got a great way to hang wreaths, holiday tote bags,
twinkle lights, and extension cords. They won't get
crushed under other decorations and they'll be easily
visible for next year.

- Get the stains out of holiday linens before putting them
away. What do you do to get rid of candle wax on your
favorite tablecloth? Remove all hardened wax with a dull
knife. Place the stain facedown on paper towels. Tackle
from the back with cleaning fluid or dry-cleaning
solvent, or treat with a solution of 1-tbsp. mild white
hand dishwashing liquid and 1 tsp. household ammonia

in 1 cup water. Then wash according to the care label in the hottest water safe for the fabric.

- This month, make it a point to clean out your clothes closet. Chances are you got some new holiday finery, so perhaps that three-year-old blouse that you never wear can finally go. If you're not quite ready to be merciless, try placing a small ribbon around the top of each of your clothes hangers. Whenever you wear an outfit, remove the ribbon. At the end of the year (or perhaps *next* New Year's Day), take any outfit that still has a ribbon and donate it to Goodwill or a resale shop.

- Plan to take advantage of the after-holiday sales in stores this week. On New Year's Day, make a list of what you need. White sales abound, and winter clothes are marked down—now is a good time to address any wardrobe deficits your closet cleaning may have uncovered.

YEARLY CALENDAR CHECK

Make a master list of birthday and/or anniversary cards you will need for the next year. Buy a few at a time when you are out shopping. Look ahead to reservations you'll need to make, invitations you may need to dispatch, and babysitters you need to book. (Line one up for Valentine's Day ASAP). Schedule teeth cleanings, yearly checkups, and oil changes.

- For great savings, buy next year's wrapping paper, ribbons, cards, boxes, and decorations.

Family

- Create a family time capsule—what better time than New Year's to institute this fun tradition? Fill a clean cookie tin with kid's drawings, family vacation photos, newspaper articles, and fun family facts. Label the top with an "open date" ten or twenty years in the future and then seal securely with duct tape.
- Sit down with your loved ones and set some family goals for the New Year. Everyone is more likely to achieve their resolutions when they have the encouragement of those around them.
- Make a resolution to get your entire family around the dinner table every night. If that's impossible, then get them together for breakfast every morning. It's been proven that children who share regular mealtimes with their parents are more communicative, more self-assured, and less likely to get into trouble than kids who don't sit down and eat with their parents.
- In addition to goal setting, use today to begin planning an active family vacation. Find out what your kids are up for—think skiing, snowboarding, snowshoeing, kayaking, hiking, or biking. Take a trip to a dude ranch or to one of our country's spectacular national parks. Consult your calendar; take a family vote, and start planning!

- Cold weather keeping the kids inside today? Take advantage of the day at home together to monitor their TV-watching habits. Watch what your kids are watching. Then resolve not to use the TV as a babysitter. Keep television sets out of children's bedrooms, set time limits, tape age-appropriate shows, turn off the TV during meals, and watch less TV as a family.
- Mark New Year's Day as "Board Game/Family Day" from now on. Continue the event one evening every month throughout the year ahead.
- If your parents or grandparents are still at your house for their holiday visit, videotape an "interview" with them. Have them answer questions about their lives, their childhoods, and their family traditions. Family stories are among the richest legacies they can leave you.

Self

- Linger in bed today! New Year's day is a day to sleep late and rouse yourself gently. Place cucumber slices on your eyes, especially if they're puffy this morning, and take some quiet time for yourself. Breathe a sigh of relief. The holiday season is over.
- Start this year with self-acceptance. When you get up this morning, look at yourself in the mirror and give yourself a compliment, out loud! Start replacing negative images of yourself with positive ones. Make this a new morning ritual.

- Try a *warm* shower today. Avoid hot showers and baths; high heat takes moisture right out of your skin. Use an exfoliating shower gel to remove any unwanted dirt, makeup, or dead skin from your body. Rinse thoroughly, then moisturize, moisturize, moisturize! Rich creams are necessary for the winter months; use petroleum-based lotions on superdry skin, and remember to apply while your skin is still damp for better absorption.

- New Year's is all about breaking old habits. So if cosmetics are an ironclad part of your morning, give your makeup a day off today (especially if you're not expecting company) and enjoy a face that feels squeaky clean. Conversely, if you normally don't use makeup . . . today's the day to put some on!

- If your hair lies limp and flat because of winter's dry air, try blow-drying your hair upside down and use hot rollers for a couple minutes right after to provide a little midwinter hair lift and bounce. To get rid of static electricity on your hair this winter, rub a clean dryer sheet over your hair.

- Before heading out for your New Year's walk, don't forget the sunscreen. Sun protection is a necessity all year round. UV rays can cut through any type of weather and are intensified by the glare from snow-covered ground. Be sure to wear sunglasses as well.

- Nourish your brain by vowing to make time for reading every day. Make a list of the twelve books you want to read this year. Consider starting a book club with friends.

- Use today to come up with one soul-enriching activity to practice throughout the year. Consider a weekday-morning walk with your girlfriend, Sunday-morning pancakes with your family, a Friday date night with your spouse, or a weekly kaffeeklatsch with your sister. Or use this month to find a hobby or a project so engrossing that you—even for a brief time—completely forget the world around you.

CHITCHAT

As one of my New Year's resolutions, I set out to find a new hobby. I wanted to create with my hands, so I attended a range of alternative art workshops at our local craft center, like pottery and jewelry making. Quite unexpectedly, I found two crafts that I became thoroughly passionate about . . . the art of stained-glass making and hand-beading. How much richer these new-found pastimes have made my life! These hobbies also helped me to make many gifts for friends and family. Moreover, in the course of my search for a new creative outlet, I've met wonderful people and made many new friends.

—Linda McClintock

- Since you probably stayed up late last night, try to tuck yourself in early this evening. Lack of sleep not only impairs concentration, physical performance, and memory, but it can also lead to serious problems, like depression and heart disease. Sleep boosts immune function, enhances metabolism, and helps you maintain a good mood. It has been proven that when you are well rested, you can resist unhealthy foods more easily and maintain your willpower.

- If you have trouble sleeping, try one of these remedies: Before going to bed, take a minute to write down your thoughts and literally get them off your mind. Try to curb your caffeine consumption during the day. If your friendly feline is waking you up during the night, keep the animals out. Turn your clock face so you don't see it. How comfortable is your mattress? Perhaps it's time for a new one. Is your partner's snoring keeping you awake? Sew a tennis ball on the back of his pajamas or nightshirt; most people snore while lying on their back and this might prevent him from doing that. Sip warm milk, which contains sleep-inducing tryptophan.

Grace Notes
for January . . .

Martin Luther King Day

A day to honor the birth date of the civil rights leader
who fought to bring racial equality, freedom, and
justice to everyone in our country.

Health

Dig through your cookbooks or go online and find some
healthy recipes for soul food tonight. Try spicy jerk chicken,
sweet potatoes, and collard greens—just be sure to leave out
the salt pork and bacon.

Fitness

Gospel music played an important part in the civil rights
movement. Tune in to its inspiration and energy by playing
some this evening as you make dinner. Start a marching
procession with your kids through the kitchen. If you're

looking for more strenuous exercise, sign up for an African dance or hip-hop class at your local Y.

Home

Purchase a peace lily for your coffee table.

Family

During tonight's dinner conversation, discuss Dr. King's legacy. Even if your kids are too young to understand the particulars of the civil rights movement, it's never too early to discuss concepts like bravery, fairness, and equality. Have each family member share ideas about what he or she could do to promote positive change for the future. Check out a book on Dr. King or Rosa Parks from the library and read it together before bedtime.

Self

Nourish your soul today by reaching out to others. Open the phone book to the Government and Community sections, make a call, and plan some volunteer time for a charity of your choice.

Chinese New Year

The Chinese New Year is celebrated on the first day of
the first moon of the Chinese lunar calendar;
it may fall at any time between January 21 and
February 19. The fifteen-day celebration is the most
important, colorful, and elaborate of Chinese festivals,
and is marked by family feasts and rich traditions.

Health

Prepare a healthy Asian feast tonight. Serve long noodles for
long life (be sure not to cut them); steam fresh vegetables—
bamboo shoots are a New Year's favorite—and a whole fish to
represent togetherness, or a chicken for prosperity. Accompany with brown rice and Chinese tea, and you've got a feast
fit for an emperor!

Fitness

In honor of the holiday, experiment with a martial art. Not
convinced you're the next Jackie Chan? Try tai chi; it's gentle, invigorating, and profoundly centering. You can find a

class at your local gym or community center, or rent a video-tape.

Home

Buy a live, blooming plant. According to Chinese tradition, flowering plants symbolize rebirth and new growth. A plant that blossoms on New Year's Day heralds a year of prosperity. Place a bowl of tangerines and oranges on your table; tangerines are a symbol of good luck, and oranges stand for wealth.

Family

Check the newspaper or go online and find out your family's Chinese birth signs. The Chinese zodiac developed out of an ancient folk tradition of nicknaming the repeating cycle of twelve years: Rat, Ox, Tiger, Rabbit, Dragon, Snake, Horse, Sheep, Monkey, Rooster, Dog, and Pig. Are you a patient, easygoing Ox married to a charming, mischievous Monkey?

Self

Today, observe some Chinese customs: Avoid using scissors or any sharp objects today lest you cut the threads of luck. Avoid arguments or any sort of negative language today—it's considered very bad luck! And finally, slip on those red shoes hidden in the back of your closet or pull on that red sweater. Red is the Chinese color for luck!

February

Valentine's Day

According to one legend, Valentine was a third-century Christian priest who defied Emperor Claudius's decree that forbade soldiers from marrying (he thought single men made better warriors) by performing secret wedding ceremonies for love-struck young couples. For his disobedience to the empire he was made a martyr, and for his commitment to commitment he was made a saint. A competing legend holds that Valentine was an imprisoned man who fell in love with his jailer's daughter. The note that he sent her, signed, "Your Valentine," was the world's first valentine.

Health

- Cue up some dreamy dinner music tonight! Listening to slow music during meals can help you eat 40 percent less, according to studies at Johns Hopkins University. "Adagio" music calms the nervous system and improves mood, making it easier to eat at a leisurely pace. Moreover, you give your brain time to register "I'm full" signals before the meal is complete.
- If you and your valentine have dinner reservations tonight (you'd better have made them early, as it's one of the most popular restaurant date nights of the year!), ask the waiter not to bring you the breadbasket. If it's not there it can't tempt you.

- Snack on grapes today, which were, according to the ancient Romans, the food of love. Substituting any variety of grapes for a high-fat, high-sodium snack like chips will not only save you calories; it will also supply you with a host of healthy nutrients, including potassium, vitamin C, fiber, flavonoids, and iron. Grapes are rated one of the top ten antioxidant foods; they protect against cancer and help the blood vessels remain open and flexible.
- Good news for Valentine's Day: chocolate's not all bad. Chocolate contains less then one-tenth of the caffeine in coffee and it also contains phenylethylamine (PEA), which is suspected to be the brain chemical that spikes when you're in love. PEA is a stimulant and mood stabilizer. Also, chocolate is made with lecithin, a kind of fat that is actually good for you!
- February is national Heart Awareness Month, and a good time to remember that heart disease is the leading cause of death among American women. Make sure your ticker is in top shape by having your doctor do an assessment of your health risk factors, including blood pressure, body mass index, pulse, cholesterol profile, and glucose levels. Testing for these things can determine your chance of developing cardiovascular disease in the next ten years.

**SIMPLE SUGGESTIONS FOR
CELEBRATORY MEALS**

Valentine's Day is a great time to be creative. Serve up a sensual meal that will have your honey licking his lips for more. Try this red-themed meal: shrimp cocktail, linguini with vodka sauce (toss in lobster or shrimp), red leaf salad, and a low-fat cream-cheese cake drizzled with a strawberry puree. For dessert, try pink champagne, chocolate-dipped strawberries, chocolate cake with raspberries, chocolate truffles, chocolate-covered cherries, or even hot chocolate spiked with your favorite liqueur.

Fitness

- Congratulations! You've been sticking to your fitness routine. For demonstrating such commitment, reward yourself with an extra special valentine—a gym membership.
- Blend fitness with romance this February 14 and dance! Ask your sweetie to accompany you to a class or rent a videotape. Depending on your tastes, you can waltz or foxtrot, salsa or swing, or even tango—those deep lunges do wonders for your thighs. Don't despair if your spouse won't dance. Go solo! Try ballet, belly dancing, tap, jazz, or hip-hop. It's no coincidence that dancers are lean and lithe—so sign up at a local studio (there are plenty of classes for adult beginners) or rent a video.

FITNESS FOCUS: CARDIO

In the spirit of Heart Awareness Month, make cardio training your February focus.

- Train heart smart. Calculate your target heart rate by subtracting your age from 220. Multiply the sum by 80 percent, and you've got your maximum heart rate. (For example, if you're thirty years old, subtract 30 from 220, which gives you 190. 190 multiplied by .80 equals 152. When exercising, try to bring your heart rate to 152 beats per minute.) You can calculate beats per minute by pressing two fingers (not your thumb) to the carotid artery in your neck. If you count beats in a minute right now, you'll have your resting heart rate.
- If you're serious about improving your cardiovascular health or simply like gadgets, consider investing in a heart-rate monitor. These devices strap onto your arm or chest, and they measure your heart rate through your workout, enabling you to know *exactly* how hard you're working. Prices start at a hundred dollars, but they can be a great motivator.
- Speaking of motivation, nothing works better to spur you to sweat than a workout you enjoy. This month, in addition to your morning walk, experiment with one new form of cardio training every week at your gym. Try swimming, spinning, kickboxing, step classes, jumping rope, jogging, biking, rowing, or climbing and see if you fall in love. Your heart will love you for it!

- On Valentine's Day, ask your spouse to join you in an activity (his choice) that will send both your pulses racing!

HOME Décor

- Roses are red . . . so decorate your home accordingly and you won't feel blue at all! Place a bunch of red gerbera daisies on your windowsill or a cherry-colored figurine on your nightstand. According to the ancient Chinese design philosophy of feng shui, red is the color used to attract wealth, prosperity, and luck.
- If romance is what you're looking to attract, put red sheets or a red heart-shaped pillow on your bed— something that signifies love.
- Decorate your dinner table with a red table runner and a fresh-flower/floating-candle centerpiece. Fill a shallow bowl with water; add several large, individual blooms and floating candles. Red pillar candles and red and white accent flowers on either side of the centerpiece will complete the look and radiate romance.
- Hang a heart-shaped wreath on your door. Show the world that you are honoring this day with love to share.
- Be sure to light a fire in your fireplace this evening. If you don't have a fireplace, re-create that flickering, flattering glow by lighting candles throughout your home.

FUN FACTS:
VALENTINE'S DAY ROSES

A red rose means "love," and is the flower of Eros, or the little winged fellow we know as Cupid. A white rose represents purity and spiritual love; it is the flower of the Virgin Mary. Yellow roses mean joy and gladness. Coral roses signify desire. Orange roses indicate fascination and enthusiasm. Lavender roses represent love at first sight. Light pink roses suggest admiration, grace, and gentility. Dark pink roses say, "Thank you." Pale-colored roses mean friendship. The rose has been around for at least 35 million years. Fossil specimens have been found in Colorado, Oregon, and Montana in the United States.

- Make and hang a Valentine's Day shadow-box gift. In a store-bought shadow box (available in any craft store), place twelve silk roses and label each rose with one of the following: "This rose is for long friendship, this for unconditional love, this for financial wealth, this for everlasting happiness, this for success, this for knowledge, this for beauty—both inner and outer, this for family, this for honesty, this for a long and healthy life, this for me, and the final one, for you."

HOMEkeeping and Organization

- Purchase your Valentine's Day cards early in the month for best selection. Don't forget to send one to all the valentines in your life . . . your dad, a special friend, child, or godmother, etc. For an extra-special gesture, consider making your own Valentine's Day cards.

- As Valentine's Day approaches, make it a point to spruce up your bedroom. You spend more than one-third of your life in this room, which represents sleep, relaxation, and intimacy—so honor it. Put anything lying on the floor in its proper place. Get all the dust bunnies out from under your bed; move your furniture to vacuum beneath and behind it. As you do, cast a critical eye at the contents of the room that *should* be your sanctuary. Be sure that everything in it, whether a piece of furniture or a framed print, is something that you love. If you don't love it, move it or toss it.

- No proper bedroom cleaning is complete without an effort to organize dresser drawers. In honor of the holiday, have a heart and donate all clothes that no longer fit to your local women's shelter. Remember, getting rid of all of your too-big outfits means saying good-bye to that particular size *for good*. If you think you may again fit into too-small clothes, place these clothes in a box and put the box away. Try them on every three months. If they don't fit within nine months, give them away.

- Make your bed, and then make it smell heavenly by scenting your linens today! Squirt a few cotton balls with your favorite perfume, and then tuck them into your linen closet. As the perfume evaporates, its fragrance lingers on sheets and towels.

- Before you get all dolled up for your date with your honey, clean out your cosmetics drawer, and make this a Valentine's Day ritual. It's fine to get teary-eyed on this sentimental holiday, but you don't want your eyes to go red on account of vintage mascara! Wash your applicators, brushes, and sponges. Throw away any mascara that you've had for more than three months, as well as any makeup that has separated or has developed an odd odor. If you can't remember how long ago you bought it or the last time you wore it, throw it out. Take stock and make sure you have the essentials: concealer (one shade lighter than your foundation), foundation, eyelash curler, a duo eye shadow—a light color to highlight and a darker shade for just above the crease of the eyelid—eyeliner, brow pencil and brush, mascara, blush, and a lipstick.
- To remove any Valentine's Day chocolate from clothing, first scrape away the chocolate and blot the spot with cool water. Presoak using powdered laundry detergent with enzymes, following label directions. If necessary, treat with 1 tsp. household ammonia diluted in 1 cup water (but don't do this for wool or silk blends). Rinse and launder as usual.
- Defog a cloudy vase for your Valentine's Day roses! Just fill the vase with water, then drop in two Alka-Seltzer tablets. Let them dissolve, and then rinse. The citric

acid and sodium bicarbonate react with the spot to lift the stain from the glass. Then fill your sparkling-clean vase with flowers and enjoy!

- On a less romantic note, by February you should have received all W-2, W-9, and income-reporting documentation. Reduce stress (and help your heart) by not waiting until the last minute to file. Use February 14 as the date by which you will have assembled your income tax arsenal. Gather all pertinent forms, receipts, and materials and file by month's end.

MONTHLY CALENDAR CHECK

- Planning on going out for some Saint Patty's Day fun next month? It's a good idea to book your dinner reservations now. Don't forget to invite a few close friends . . . it's a fun night to party!
- February is Heart Awareness Month, making it a good time to book doctors' appointments.

Family

- Help your children write out their Valentine's Day cards. Whether the cards are store-bought or homemade, few rituals are more fun for kids (who *love* to get mail) than exchanging them with friends. Find out whether your kids' classes have Valentine's Day "mailboxes," and if children are expected to have cards for everyone, or if possible exclusions could cause hurt feelings.

- Create a Valentine's Day tree of good deeds to encourage your family to follow the Random Acts of Kindness movement. Start by cutting a tree—sans the leaves—out of construction paper, along with some cutout hearts. With each good deed you do in the month of February, paste a piece of heart-shaped foliage to the branches. See how big your tree can grow!
- Make baskets of love for everyone in your family. Fill the baskets with a book, chocolate, stuffed animal, card, or anything you feel that special person would adore. Have the basket waiting outside their bedroom door in the morning, or at their seat at the kitchen table.
- Spend quality time with your partner. As part of your Valentine's celebration, write down three "dates" that you'd like to go on. Share your ideas; pick the ones you both like the best and start scheduling them into your calendars.
- Trade foot massages with your significant other! Not only is it soothing, but reflexologists are using it to help treat depression. According to traditional Chinese medicine, at the center of your foot, right below the ball, is the "bubbling spring." Rub this point, then massage along the arch from heel to toes.
- Wear something of your spouse's today (a T-shirt, socks, or hat, etc.) and perhaps even a tiny dab of his favorite cologne. This way you can stay connected with him all day.
- Make love the topic of your dinner conversation. How many movies or books can you think of with the word

---

FUN FACTS: VALENTINE'S DAY

Each year, the average American man spends $122 on Valentine's Day gifts. The average woman spends $50.

"love" in the title? How many songs can you sing that contain the word "love"? Teach your family how to say "I love you" in different languages. French: *Je t'aime* (zheh tem); Italian: *Ti amo* (tee ah-mo); German: *Ich liebe dich* (eesh lee-beh deesh); Romanian: *Te iubesc* (the you-besk).

- Hug your children and tell them you love them today. Children who have their mother's physical and emotional love grow up with strong self-esteem. Girls who had a strong bond with their mothers are less likely to have an eating disorder and have a better body image, according to Anne Madeleine Hahn-Smith, Ph.D., and Jane Ellen Smith, Ph.D., of the University of New Mexico.

Self

- Give yourself a rosy-red Valentine's Day facial! Strawberries are high in vitamin C and also make a great face pack for oily skin. Mash a few strawberries with a fork, add a bit of honey to hold the berries

together, apply to face, and then rinse. For dry winter
skin, mash a banana with a fork, mix in a bit of honey to
make a paste, and put on your face. Wait ten minutes
and rinse off.

- Think pink in unusual ways. Pepto-Bismol makes a great
face mask for sensitive skin. Just as it coats and soothes
your stomach, it softly caresses the skin. Apply with a
cotton ball, allow to dry, and rinse with cool water.

- For a natural red coat of "lipstick," try dabbing a Q-tip
into the powder form of cherry flavored gelatin and
apply to your lips. Let the powder sit for five minutes,
then lick it off. Try this on your daughters too; they'll
love it!

- Start every conversation this Valentine's Day by sharing
a compliment. Kindness has a ripple effect, and you'll
touch more people than you can imagine.

- February 14 isn't *just* about romance, so make a heartfelt
gesture and reestablish old connections. Get in touch
with an old friend, or, if there's an issue that needs to be
addressed, resolve a rankling hurt. What better day to
exercise forgiveness and compassion than a day devoted
to the heart?

- Sit back with a cup of antioxidant green tea and read
your favorite poems aloud. Not only will declaiming a
beloved sonnet soothe you, it can actually slow your
heart to match the rhythm of the poem. According to a
July 2002 article published in the *International Journal of
Cardiology*, reading poetry out loud has been shown to
improve vagal tone. (The vagus is the nerve that

regulates heart rate; high or good vagal tone is
associated with a heart that can recuperate from stress.
Low vagal tone is associated with a heightened risk of
heart attack or stroke.)

- Perk up for puckering up! Exfoliate your lips by gently
brushing them with a toothbrush and use a lip balm to
moisturize. Do not lick your lips; your saliva will only
dehydrate them.

- Take a romantic bath with your loved one today. Relax
with him in a chamomile-tea bath with rose petals, and
follow with a sensuous massage with lavender oil.

Grace Notes
for February . . .

Observed on the third Monday in February, this
federal holiday began as a celebration of
George Washington's birthday on his last year in
office, but has since been expanded to include
President Abraham Lincoln's birthday.

Health

The story of Washington and the cherry tree may be a myth,
but cherries' antioxidant properties are for real. Top this
morning's high-fiber cereal with a handful of vitamin-rich
dried cherries.

Fitness

Head out on a Presidents' Day ski trip! The day off makes it a
perfect opportunity to get some great outdoor exercise. Pack
up your ski/snowboard equipment and head for the hills.

Home

Make an executive decision this Presidents' Day and get rid of one household item that you never liked.

Family

Before dinner tonight, look up a few fun historical facts about past presidents. Write trivia questions on index cards and place one at each table setting to spark a fun and educational dinner conversation.

Self

In honor of our first president, tuck away two one-dollar bills in your piggy bank every day. Keep this going and see what Washington can do for you!

Super Bowl Sunday

An honorary holiday that has become
a traditional celebration in America for the
gridiron aficionado and fair-weather fan alike.

Health

For an easy main dish that will keep you out of the kitchen,
use a Crock-Pot to cook up some savory turkey chili. Nothing goes better with corn bread, good friends, and a good
game of football! Be sure to add lots of beans to up your fiber
intake.

Fitness

With every first down, do a set of knee-ups to target abs and
outer thighs. Sitting in a sturdy chair with feet flat on the
floor and knees at a ninety-degree angle, press your lower

back firmly into the chair. Then tighten your abs, and bring your right knee up toward your chest. Hold for ten seconds, and then lower to the ground. Repeat with your left leg. Do three sets.

Home

Use paper plates, napkins, and cups in the colors of the two opposing teams (this makes identifying team allegiances, not to mention cleanup, a breeze!). If you are hosting a party, create a social space with the buffet table and bar well away from the television, so avid football fans won't be distracted by the folks more interested in conversation than in two-point conversions!

Family

Play an NFL trivia game with your family. Today's sports page should provide an adequate source of Super Bowl stats and football facts.

Self

If you choose to drink today, alternate alcoholic beverages with sparkling water garnished with a wedge of lemon or lime.

March

Saint Patrick's Day

Saint Patrick, the patron saint of Ireland, was born in
Wales about AD 385. Kidnapped into slavery by Irish
marauders, he became a Christian while working as
a lonely laborer in Ireland. Six years after his
capture, he escaped enslavement and entered the
priesthood. He then returned to Ireland, embarking
on a thirty-year mission to convert the Irish to
Catholicism. His feast day on March 17 was originally
a religious holiday, but has since evolved to become
a celebration of all things Irish. Saint Patrick's Day was
first celebrated in the United States in Boston in 1737.

Health

- Capture the colors of the Irish flag in an easy snack.
  Serve bright orange baby carrots on a bed of greens. Just
  be sure to pass up the pale carrots in the produce aisle.
  According to the U.S. Department of Agriculture's
  Research Service, darker orange carrots provide up to 50
  percent more beta-carotene, an antioxidant that's
  converted by the body into vitamin A and helps reduce
  the risk of heart disease and some cancers.
- Too much stout can make *you* stout. Although according
  to Irish lore—and advertising—"Guinness Is Good for
  You," a pint has 210 calories. Keep that in mind as you
  toast, "Erin Go Bragh" ("Long live Ireland").

- If your heart is set on a traditional Irish dinner of corned beef and cabbage, complete with green beer, then go for it. Just remember to eat in moderation. Try filling your plate with vegetables first; then go back for corned beef. Eating in this manner will help prevent you from overindulging.

SIMPLE SUGGESTIONS FOR CELEBRATORY MEALS

In Ireland, Saint Patrick's Day was long considered a holy day. Pubs were closed and there were no raucous Saint Patty's day parades wending their way through the streets. Rather, it is Irish-Americans who are responsible for many of the traditions with which we mark Saint Patrick's feast day, including that favorite of leprechauns in Boston, New York, and Chicago, corned beef and cabbage. Traditional *Irish* foods include boiled ham and cabbage or bacon and cabbage. For your celebration, you might also consider serving one of the following Hibernian favorites: broiled lamb chops, smoked or poached salmon, Irish stew, or braised root vegetables. End the meal with Irish scones or fruity Irish soda bread and a generous cup of Irish coffee.

Fitness

- Saint Patrick's Day marks the end of winter. It's a great time to tune up your walking routine. If you've been walking since January, switch to a more challenging route.

- Saint Patrick's Day also signifies the start of spring cleaning. Play some fun, lively music (perhaps an Irish reel!) and pick up the pace as you sweep, scour, and tidy. You will get more done and burn more calories at the same time.

FITNESS FOCUS: ABDOMINALS

This Saint Patrick's Day, get rid of the pot of gold that's settled on your belly. That's right, mid-March is a great time to start working on your midsection. Beginning on Saint Patrick's Day, do the following two or three times a week.

- Squeeze in a few sets of ab crunches as you wait for your morning shower water to heat up. Lie on your bathroom throw rug, clasp your hands lightly behind your neck, and lift your chin to the ceiling. Start with just one set of eight and work up to two or three sets. Make this a lifelong before-shower habit!
- Try a tummy flattener that also improves your circulation. Lie on your back with your feet up off the ground, your knees bent and pointed toward your chest. Wrap your arms around your knees and pull them into your ribs as you press your belly and back firmly into the mat. Slowly lift your head to look toward your belly. Breathe. Hold for a count of eight. Try to work up to three reps.
- Try this Pilates move. To begin, lie flat on your back with your arms stretched out on the floor alongside you. Keeping your lower back pressed firmly on the floor, lift

your hands and reach toward your toes. Keep your chin tucked against your chest, so that your back creates a C curve. With your legs straight, your knees and ankles pressed together, and your toes turned out, lift your legs to a forty-five-degree angle from the floor (about six to eight inches off the ground). Start pumping your arms up and down as if you were slapping the floor without actually hitting it. Continue for a count of eight. Work up to three sets. Beginners can keep their feet on the ground.

HOME Décor

- Make a lucky Irish wall hanging for your Saint Patrick's Day celebration. Paint a rainbow on a large sheet of rollable paper (butcher paper is good). Hang your mural on the wall, and have your children or party guests sign it and write down one wish. Reuse every Saint Patrick's Day, and have fun reading last year's wishes.
- Mail or hand-deliver invitations to your upcoming Saint Patrick's bash. Sprinkle some green confetti in the envelopes, and include a temporary shamrock tattoo for your guests to help them get into the spirit.
- Dress up your table with a traditional green tablecloth. Or try a white tablecloth sprinkled with shiny green confetti. Use plastic tablecloths for quick cleanup.
- Create festive place settings with mini plastic pots of gold. Write guests' names on green craft paper, roll up,

and place inside pots. Or use permanent marker and write the names of your guests on green plastic Saint Patrick's Day top hats.

- Cut shamrocks out of green craft paper, then hang, scatter, and tape them everywhere! Suspend some green balloons from the ceiling lamp over your table. Stick some Irish flags into a plant and create a Patty party centerpiece.
- Create large shamrocks to use as place mats on your dinner table during Saint Patrick's week. Have the kids help you decorate them using paints, stamps, or markers.
- Turn green top hats upside down and fill them with snacks such as peanuts, chips, and pretzels.
- Think spring green! This week, take some time out with your indoor houseplants and make certain they're in peak condition. Water, prune, and toss as necessary.

HOMEkeeping and Organization

- After the long winter, use Saint Patrick's Day as the starting point for beginning to plan this year's garden. Look through seed catalogs and decide what you want to plant in your vegetable and flower gardens. Now is the time to order your seeds to start sowing indoors later this month.
- Immediately following Saint Patrick's Day is a great time to begin shopping for a new grill. You can get a great deal

on last year's model, or if you prefer, first choice of the latest editions.

- Grab a pad, pen, and your datebook. Today's the day to plan spring cleanup projects all around the house. If Saint Patrick could convert all of Ireland, then surely you can transform your house! Sit down with your family and map out both major and minor cleanup jobs. Then create a task list and ask every member of your family (no matter how young) to volunteer to help with one job a week. Remember, spring cleaning is the time for jobs you don't do on a weekly basis. Here are some suggestions:

  - Dust, vacuum, and wipe down all radiators, heat registers, and ceiling fans. Have furnace and air conditioning systems serviced. Clean out fireplaces and have the chimney professionally cleaned. Clean fireplace bricks by scrubbing with full-strength white household vinegar.

  - Wash out all trash bins and line with plastic bags. Store your extra plastic grocery bags in the bottom of the can for quick reloading.

  - Scrub the bathroom. Take down the shower-curtain liner and launder. Don't forget to clean your medicine cabinet. Discard all prescription medicines that are no longer necessary. Check the dates on all over-the-counter medicines and discard all the outdated ones.

  - Don't forget your basement, attic, or garage. This March, make your Saint Patrick's Day wish to get organized come true. Aim to spend at least one hour getting control of your storage space each week. Start in one corner and begin to work your way around, making piles of things you want to donate, sell, and keep. Set a timer each day and clean for an hour or another preset length of time. Or you can use the trash-bag method: Bring one or two trash bags into your attic each time you go in and don't stop working until you fill the bags.

- Plan an after-spring-cleaning yard sale. Designate one area of your home as the place to collect sale items. Tag and clean items up for better selling.

FUN FACTS: SPRING CLEANING!

Eighty percent of Americans clean out their refrigerators at least four times annually. Fifty-five percent clean out their closets that often. Forty-two percent of Americans clean out their medicine cabinets at least once a season, and 63 percent report having outdated medicines on their shelves.

Family

- Dress the entire family in green and begin taking an annual Saint Patrick's Day photo of your own clan. Start a special Saint Patrick's Day photo album.
- A week or two before Saint Patty's day, fill a paper cup with soil and grass seeds and have your children draw

---

FUN FACTS: SAINT PATRICK'S DAY

Three is Ireland's magic number—hence the legend of the shamrock. Numbers played an important role in Celtic symbolism. Three was the most sacred and magical number. Three may have signified totality: past, present, and future, or sky, earth, and underworld.

---

and cut out a leprechaun face. Tape it to the front of the cup, and watch your leprechaun grow hair!

- Start a new tradition this year and serve green milk with breakfast. Just tint regular milk with a drop or two of green food coloring.
- Throw a lively all-ages party this Saint Patrick's Day; it's a great excuse to have friends and family over. Set an Irish mood with festive Irish folk music, rent *Riverdance*, and encourage kids of all ages to have an Irish step dancing contest.
- Have a singalong. If you can't play "Danny Boy" and "When Irish Eyes Are Smiling" on the piano, rent a karaoke machine.
- Plan a family treasure hunt. Cut shamrocks out of green construction paper and write clues leading to the pot of gold—use plastic gold coins or foil-wrapped chocolate coins.
- Get the whole family into spring decluttering! Tell the kids that they can keep the profits (another sort of green) from selling toys they no longer use at a yard sale.

READER TO READER

Last year on Saint Patrick's Day I used some washable green food coloring to leave leprechaun footprints all over the kitchen. I made the footprints by making a fist and using the pinkie side of my hand to stamp out "footprints." Use your fingertip to dot on the toes. I made it look like a little leprechaun walked all over our tile floors and countertops. The leprechaun left small gifts wrapped in shiny gold foil for my children. It was a fun surprise and my kids absolutely loved it!

—Bridget L., West Palm Beach, Florida

- Let each of your children choose a plant for your garden this year. Planting and cultivating a garden provides wonderful life lessons for young and old. If space is a problem, let your child work with you on a small container garden for your back deck or porch.

Self

- Even if you haven't kissed the blarney stone, call your sister, a cousin, or a friend who has moved away, and exercise your gift of the gab.
- Today is a great day to splurge on a onetime maid service to help you with spring-cleaning chores. You can work alongside the service professionals or let them handle

everything while you spend some quality time on
yourself.

- Wear rubber gloves to protect your hands while spring
cleaning. Slather on your favorite overnight moisturizer
before putting on gloves. When you are finished
cleaning, your hands will feel soft and smooth.

- In honor of the Irish and their long literary and poetic
tradition, go to the library and check out a book by an
Irish author. Feeling ambitious? Try James Joyce.
Poetic? Seamus Heaney or W. B. Yeats. Like a laugh *and*
a good cry? Frank McCourt. In the mood for history?
Thomas Cahill. Like a warm, small-town story? Maeve
Binchy.

- Treat yourself to a hot cup of Irish coffee today. You
deserve it.

Grace Notes
for March . . .

Mardi Gras

Mardi Gras, or Fat Tuesday, is the day of feasting and
revelry that precedes the somber season of Lent.
As a way to "get it all out" before folks
"give it all up," its boisterous traditions and
over-the-top fun are celebrated with
spectacular verve in New Orleans.

Health

Celebrate Mardi Gras with seafood jambalaya tonight! Top
brown rice with tomatoes, seafood, chicken sausage, vegetables, and sizzling Cajun spices. For dessert, serve a healthy
variation on a king cake, the traditional dessert of Mardi
Gras, by dusting an angel food cake with purple, green, and
yellow crystallized sugar. Be sure to hide a small plastic baby
inside—the person who gets the baby has to furnish next
year's king cake.

Fitness

In honor of the holiday, both you and the saints can go "marching in" when you dance to the raucous strains of Dixieland jazz.

Home

From your local grocer or florist, bring home a bouquet of fresh flowers to brighten up your kitchen table. Purple, gold, and green are Mardi Gras colors.

Family

Spread out some newspapers and fashion some festive Mardi Gras masks. Use construction paper, sequins, glitter, feathers—the more outrageous the better! Who needs New Orleans when you can have a backyard parade?

Self

Tonight, trade your Mardi Gras feathered masterpiece for an invigorating honey-banana mask! Mash ½ banana with 1 tbsp. of honey. Apply to your face and let dry for ten minutes before rinsing.

Lent

In Christian liturgy, this forty-day period stretching
from Ash Wednesday to Easter Sunday is one
of penitence and reflection. It is traditional to eat
no meat on Fridays, and give up a favorite food or
drink as an exercise of spiritual discipline.

Health

Give up refined sugar this month. It's a tough habit to break,
but you'll feel better. Go for it!

Fitness

Cut back TV watching by one hour every day. Changing
sedentary habits for Lent is a good way to introduce more
healthful habits into your routine.

Home

Think simplicity. Look at your shelves, tables, and windowsills and stow away a few knickknacks.

Family

Designate a family money jar in the kitchen to collect spare change for each day of Lent and donate the accumulated money to your church or favorite charity.

Self

Even if you don't observe Lent as a religious holiday, it's worth noting that it's a time set aside for introspection. Reserve some quiet time for yourself and try meditating for at least ten minutes a day throughout Lent.

April

Easter

According to Christian tradition, Easter Sunday marks the day of Christ's resurrection. In order to protect themselves from persecution, second-century Christians timed their observance of the holiday to coincide with the pagan festival honoring Eostre, the great mother goddess of the Anglo-Saxons. Many of the traditional symbols of Easter—the rabbit, the egg, and even the lily—are ancient symbols of fertility.

Health

- Keep your Easter eggs cool! Refrigeration slows bacterial growth, so it's important to refrigerate all decorated eggs and egg-containing foods.
- Tune in to feelings of hunger and satiety during this religious holiday season. Eat only when your stomach growls or you have a hollow feeling. Stop when you are comfortable . . . not full.
- Fill Easter baskets with trinkets and toys for your children rather than traditional chocolate and candy.
- Good news! You need not skip the traditional holiday ham: Ham is a good low-fat source of protein. A three-ounce serving of extra lean ham contains approximately

---

CHITCHAT

Evenings are the hardest time for me to stick with my healthy eating program. On nights when I feel especially hungry and want to munch, I give myself a manicure or put on a facial mask. The thirty minutes it takes to do these things gives me time to forget about my cravings. It's also a treat to spend this time on me!

—Beverly Zingarella

---

116 calories, 4 grams of fat, 25 milligrams of cholesterol, 18 grams of protein, and 965 grams of sodium. When selecting the type or size of your Easter ham, think in terms of servings per pound rather than price per pound when comparing values. Remember, it's the *edible* servings that count. Bone-in ham (sold as whole ham, half ham, shank and butt half, or center slices) provides two to three servings per pound. Boneless ham, made from sectioned pieces of lean cured meat with the external fat trimmed away, provides four to five servings per pound. Semiboneless ham, which includes the round leg or shank bone, provides three to four servings per pound.

· Be creative with leftover ham. For breakfast, stir diced ham into scrambled eggs, or mix cubed ham into corn-muffin batter and bake. Add chopped ham to diced potatoes and onions, for a hearty hash. For a quick

Easter Monday dinner, serve individual chef's salads. Top lettuce with ham, tomatoes, mushrooms, onions, and chopped hard-cooked eggs. Add ham to homemade pizza. Stir cubed ham into soups or thread onto skewers with vegetables and pineapple.

FUN FACTS: EASTER SWEETS

- Sixty million chocolate Easter bunnies are produced each year.
- According to a recent survey of American children, 74 percent believe chocolate bunnies should be eaten ears first; 13 percent said bunnies should be eaten feet first; while 10 percent favored eating the tail first.
- In 2000, Americans spent nearly $1.9 billion on Easter candy.
- Americans consume 15 million jelly beans at Easter. If all the jelly beans were lined side by side, they would circle the globe nearly three times. Favorite Easter jelly-bean flavors are cherry (20 percent), strawberry (12 percent), grape (10 percent), lime (7 percent), and blueberry (6 percent).

**SIMPLE SUGGESTIONS FOR
CELEBRATORY MEALS**

Easter is a time for new beginnings. The traditional main course for Easter is ham, which is symbolic of great joy and abundance. An Easter table is also laden with butter (often shaped into a lamb or the sign of the cross) to remind celebrants of the goodness of Jesus; colorfully decorated eggs, which represent new life and resurrection; red beets mixed with horseradish, which represent the passion of Christ; and wine and bread for Christ's blood and body. Other traditional foods include sweet breads such as hot cross buns.

Fitness

· Take a cue from ol' Peter Cottontail and try hopping toward health. Jumping rope is an outstanding form of aerobic activity. A jump rope provides a total body workout that burns more calories than walking or jogging. Better yet, it's inexpensive and small enough to fit into an Easter basket. Make sure your rope is heavy enough to help you maintain a steady rhythm. Your rope is the right length if you can stand on it and have its handles reach your armpits. Wear a good pair of sneakers, and jump on a surface with plenty of give. Begin with three three-minute increments, and try to build from there to three five-minute increments.
· Spring is here, which means it's baseball season!

Assemble your own home team and head out to the local softball field. Better yet, consider joining an adult softball league this month, and have fun as you burn fat.

· Renew your commitment to standing tall. Good posture strengthens muscles that can grow weak and strained from years of slouching. Our spines are made up of thirty-three vertebrae sandwiched between fibrous disks. They contain three normal curves: one at our neck, upper back, and lower back. Don't allow these natural curves to become stretched or compressed. If necessary, have a doctor evaluate your posture to help you make the corrections. Better posture will not only make you appear straighter, taller, and slimmer, it may help relieve daily aches and pains.

FITNESS FOCUS: GLUTES

Having a round, full tail is fine for Easter rabbits, but less charming in humans.

· Check out some fitness videos in the week preceding Easter and make it a point to concentrate on exercises that sculpt and tighten your glutes. *Buns of Steel* is a classic.

· Adding hills to your walking routine is a good way to get a lean, firm derriere.

· Blast the buttocks with an old standby—lunges. Use a fitness ball or chair and work deep into the muscle. Facing away from the chair or fitness ball, stand about two feet in front of it and place your right foot (shoelaces down) on the ball or chair behind you. With your weight

on your left foot, bend your left knee and lower your
right knee to the floor as far as you can while keeping it
in line with your toes. Pause and return to starting
position. Repeat eight to twelve times, and switch legs.
Build up to three sets.

HOME Décor

- Easter bonnets adorned with flowers and colored eggs
  make a beautiful centerpiece for your holiday table. Grab
  your glue gun and an old Easter bonnet (even one of the
  kids' will do) and have your children help you decorate
  using fresh or silk flowers, basket grass, colorful jelly
  beans, and real or plastic colored eggs. Decorate a
  second Easter bonnet for your front door!
- To blow out an egg, use a pin to carefully make small
  holes in the top and bottom of the egg. While holding
  the egg above a bowl to catch the yolk and white, blow
  through one hole. Once hollow, dry eggs out thoroughly
  and color as usual.
- Create colored eggs using all-natural egg dye. Put the
  eggs in small pots and cover with water. Add ¼ cup of
  cranberry juice for red; ¼ tsp. turmeric for yellow;
  ¼ orange peel for orange; ¼ cup blueberries for blue; or
  ¼ cup grape juice for purple. Bring to boil. Stir in 1 tsp.
  of white vinegar and let boil for one minute; remove
  from heat. Let eggs sit for fifteen minutes, then remove.
- Pick some fresh daffodils or tulips from your garden or

CHITCHAT

Growing up, I always knew Easter was near when my mom began "blowing out" eggs for an Easter egg tree. About a week before Easter Sunday, she would place three or four branches from a pussy willow tree in a vase of water (so they could root and be replanted later). Using loops of colorful pipe cleaner threaded through the top holes of the blown-out eggs, she would hang eggs, small bunnies, colorful ribbons, and other Easter decorations from the branches of the pussy willow. I have continued this tradition with my children. The tree is great fun to create, and the pretty table decoration bears the personal touch of every member of my family!

—Beverly Zingarella

buy some from a local store. Place a few flowers at each place setting on the Easter table. This will remind your guests of the Easter message of renewal, beauty, and hope.

- Two weeks before Easter, create Easter-grass place settings. Wash out empty milk cartons and cut off the tops. Cover each carton with contact paper or construction paper and decorate with markers or stickers. Fill ⅔ full with potting soil, and then generously cover with grass seed. Watered daily, the grass should grow in about four to seven days. Place a decorated egg in each carton. And write guests' names on decorated milk cartons.

· Purple and gold are the traditional Easter colors, but if you prefer a paler palette, decorate your table in pastel shades of yellow, lavender, blue, and green. Try using squares of wheatgrass as a centerpiece.

· Recycle an old Easter basket. Remove the handle and use it in the bathroom to hold soaps, potpourri, or other small items.

HOMEkeeping and Organization

· When the time "springs forward" this month, change the batteries in your smoke alarms. You should change the batteries every six months. Likewise, check the gauge on your fire extinguisher every six months.

· Easter weekend is a great time to put down your spring fertilizer for a lush green lawn this summer.

· Easter also marks the beginning of perennial season. Plant perennials, including roses, this month. Pull mulch away as spring-blooming bulbs (crocus, daffodils, and tulips) emerge from the earth. As the earth thaws, divide overgrown perennials to stimulate vitality and create new plantings. Water perennials thoroughly a few days before dividing. Replant sections at the same depth as the original plant.

· In mid-April, plant your seedlings. If your local climate demands, start tomatoes, eggplants, and peppers indoors. Use a good-quality potting mix and be sure to keep it moist and warm. You may choose to cover seed trays with clear plastic wrap to insulate until sprouts begin. In mild climates, sow seeds directly in the garden. Sow peas, lettuce, and other greens as soon as the soil can be worked.

- Continue spring cleaning! To fluff your carpet in spots where the feet or legs of your furniture have flattened it, place a small piece of ice in each dent. Allow ice to melt overnight. Take a towel and dry and fluff the carpet in the morning.

Family

- Have fun making sugared eggs with the family. Roll a dry, hard-cooked white egg in a beaten egg white. Sprinkle with superfine sugar and let dry on paper.
- Have each family member decorate a paper egg to represent his/her taste. Use colored construction paper to design eggs of all different sizes. Pretty lace can outline the eggs—use a glue stick to be sure the lace stays put.
- Start a new Easter tradition by planning a traditional egg hunt for neighbors, family, and friends. It's a fun, easy way to get both kids and parents together for a few hours out-of-doors.
- Or emulate a presidential tradition and hold an Easter egg roll. The White House Easter Egg Roll dates back to 1878 and President Rutherford B. Hayes.

- Head to a local park and have your kids look for the first signs of spring. Help them examine trees for buds, look for crocuses and snowdrops, or even that age-old harbinger of milder weather—Robin Redbreast!

Self

- Even if you're not planning to march in an Easter parade, treat yourself to a beautiful spring hat to celebrate this time of year.
- Get Easter's sense of renewal by getting more sleep. Early in April, begin to catch a few extra winks. With daylight savings time starting for many regions this month, you'll be losing an hour of sleep. Lack of sleep

---

FUN FACTS: EASTER

- Easter marshmallow Peeps: 32 calories, 0 grams fat, 6 grams sugar.
- Number of Peeps sold at Easter: More than 700 million.
- Most popular color and shape: Yellow chicks.
- Strangest ways to eat Peeps: Wait until they are stale; microwave them; freeze them; roast them; or put them on pizza.

can lead to stress, gastrointestinal problems, menstrual irregularities, and even heart disease.

- Save a few raw Easter eggs and use them on your hair. For soft, shiny tresses, whisk together two eggs, massage into hair, and shampoo out.
- Carry a fold-up travel toothbrush and use it after the Easter meal is over. This will help you stop nibbling!

Grace Notes
for April . . .

Passover

According to the Jewish lunar calendar,
Passover begins on the eve of the fifteenth day
of the month Nisan. The date varies from year to year
according to the English calendar, falling in March or
April. The holiday's name, Pesach, means "passing
over" or "protection" in Hebrew, and is derived from
the instructions given to Moses by God. In order to
compel the pharaoh to free the Israelites, God
unleashed a plague on Egypt that killed the firstborn
of both man and beast. To protect themselves, the
Israelites were told to mark their dwellings with lamb's
blood so that the angel of death could identify and
"pass over" their homes. After this plague, the Israelites
were freed from captivity, and made their exodus out of
Egypt. The Passover festival lasts eight days and
incorporates a host of rich traditions.

Health

Borrow a book from the library or go online to get some
healthy recipes for your Passover seder. Even the heaviest of

traditional recipes can be modified. The prohibition against leavened foods often translates into recipes that rely heavily on eggs. Bear in mind that a single egg contains 212 milligrams of cholesterol, which is close to the recommended daily limit of 300 milligrams. This Passover, replace whole eggs with egg whites in your recipe for matzo ball soup.

Fitness

Passover is a holiday that demands a great deal of cleaning. Save time and burn calories by wearing a weighted vest as you vacuum, mop, dust, and scrub.

Home

Before Passover begins, give all *chametz* (any food and drink made from wheat, barley, rye, oats, spelt, or their derivatives) to non-Jewish neighbors or friends. Or, better yet, donate it to the local soup kitchen for those in need.

Family

Passover is all about family: Whether you ask your teenage daughter to lead you in the second seder, have children act out the story of the Egyptian enslavement, or have a grown-up dress up as the prophet Elijah, think of ways to bring the holiday alive for your youngsters. Consider breaking the afikomen into as many pieces as there are children present. This will assure that all children find a piece and receive a special prize.

Self

Educate yourself on the rituals and practice of the Passover season. Let this be a time not simply to cook and clean, but to deepen your faith and better understand the history of the Jewish people.

April Fools' Day

The roots of this holiday reach back to the ancient New Year's celebrations, which were held at the start of spring. Today April Fools' is an occasion for practical jokes and affectionate laughter.

Health

Tonight, for a wholesome April Fools' prank your family will love, serve a healthy dessert first and dinner afterward. Have fun with your food—think upside-down cakes or inside-out sandwiches. Try a strawberry soup and an ice cream sandwich for dinner, followed by a slice of shepherd's pie for dessert.

Fitness

You may feel a little silly, but what better day than April Fools' to feature Mom and Dad cavorting like kids? Set up an obstacle course in your yard and give it a go. Have a wheel-barrow race, hop through tires, balance on a plank—you'll see how funny fitness can be.

Home

Prove you're no fool by using the first as your absolute dead-line for mailing in your income taxes.

Family

Make the kids giggle by wearing your clothes backward, serving breakfast on doll dishes, and renting a funny, family-friendly film.

Self

Begin April Fools' Day with a laugh! Tell a joke at the break-fast table today. Believe it or not, researchers at Stanford University found that laughing for thirty seconds produces the same aerobic benefits as exercising for three minutes on a rowing machine. You'll burn calories, strengthen abdominal muscles . . . and get happy!

May

Mother's Day

"God could not be everywhere and therefore he made mothers."
—JEWISH PROVERB

In 1914, President Woodrow Wilson declared the second Sunday of May Mother's Day. Since then, Mother's Day has become the most popular day of the year to phone home. Telephone lines record their highest traffic that day, as kids young and old call Mom to express their love.

Health

- Start a new tradition this Mother's Day by writing out a "Mom's Choice" menu for your special day. Beginning with breakfast in bed, let your family know exactly what to serve you.
- If you're dining out with family, make healthy choices from the menu. Order broiled or baked fish over fried; avoid cream-based sauces and dishes sautéed in butter. Enjoy yourself, but be sure not to overindulge. Restaurant serving sizes are larger than a single portion, so ask for a take-home bag *before* you begin eating. Divide your dinner and place half in your take-home bag.

- If you crave dessert on this special day, choose wisely. Many restaurants offer healthier and lighter desserts, including fresh fruit. If you absolutely must have something "sinful," share it with your family.
- Start taking a calcium supplement today if you don't get it from your daily diet. The effects of taking 1,200 milligrams of calcium daily include: 71 percent reduction in the risk of insulin resistance syndrome (prediabetes); 54 percent decrease in PMS symptoms, including bloat, food cravings, mood swings, fatigue, and migraines; and 35 percent reduction in the risk of osteoporosis.

SIMPLE SUGGESTIONS FOR CELEBRATORY MEALS

Spoil yourself (or your mother) today with a Mother's Day tea, complete with cucumber-and-smoked-salmon finger sandwiches, fresh fruit salad, and petit fours. For dinner, keep in mind that most moms like it light. Ask your family to serve Mom a healthy dinner of chicken kebabs, poached salmon, or a tofu-vegetable stir-fry, with asparagus, sugar snap peas, or spaghetti squash as possible sides. For dessert, angel food cake topped with Mom's favorite berries or meringue cookies dipped in chocolate are sure to be a treat.

Fitness

- Not all mothers want jewelry, flowers, or candy for Mother's Day. Hint to your hubby that this year you'd like some exercise equipment. Consider a PowerBelt—a padded lightweight belt with attached resistance bands that you can pull on as you walk. Not only will you increase the amount of calories you burn, but you will also increase the muscle tone in your arms.
- If you've got a green thumb, then do your Mother's Day morning workout in the garden. Simply pick up the pace while weeding, raking, or digging in the garden . . . you will burn more calories while getting more accomplished.
- For a great all-over exercise, take up tennis this month. A series of lessons make a fabulous Mother's Day gift: Not only will it get you outside into the gorgeous spring weather, but a solid game of tennis burns about 493 calories in just an hour.
- If a morning at the gym is more your speed, defer a lavish breakfast in bed for a festive lunch, and spend a long, leisurely morning at a yoga class, then linger in the sauna.

FITNESS FOCUS: ARMS

What can be more comforting than a mother's arms? This month, make sure they're strong and lean.

- Bicep curls. Standing with your feet hip distance apart and a slight bend in your knees, grasp weights with your

palms pointing out and your elbows pressed to your
sides. Slowly bend your elbows, curling the weight to
your shoulders, then slowly lower the weight to return to
the starting position.

· Tricep kickbacks. Stand with your feet slightly wider
than hip distance apart, with your knees soft. Keeping
your spine straight, bend slightly forward at the waist.
With 5-pound weights in your hands, and your palms
facing your body, bend your arms so that your elbows are
bent at a 90-degree angle, then straighten your arms
directly behind you. You should feel the muscles at the
backs of your arms (your triceps) working.

READER TO READER

With the winter so long in northern Vermont, Mother's
Day really marks the beginning of our warmer days. We
have a quick and simple breakfast, and then load up the
van with bikes, an array of clothing, and water bottles
and head to the Stowe bike path. It's the same drill
every year . . . we pedal the whole path, then we stop
for brunch at the restaurant of my choice. I love it! The
day is about making me happy, casual exercise that
everyone can enjoy (because that is how moms prefer
life to go), and yummy food, because filling tummies is
equal to filling souls.

—Ginny R., Burlington, Vermont

HOME Décor

- Use Mother's Day to start your garden journal. Clip pictures from magazines and catalogs and make notes of flowers, shrubs, and ground cover you want to include in your summer gardens. Look around and take into account the color of your house, focal points such as large trees, hedges, fences, and benches. Use them to harmonize along with the plant colors you select. Cool-colored plants in pastels, blues, and lavenders are soothing and calming, while hot colors in yellows, reds, and oranges convey warmth and excitement. Broad sweeps of color, with one shade diffusing into the next, are more effective than splashes of color here and there. Try combining three of the same colors with slight shade variations. Finally, anchor your color garden with beautiful green foliage in many different shades.
- In honor of your own mother, plant a rosebush in your yard, or buy a potted dwarf version for your window.
- Beginning today, fill your home and your office with masses of fresh flowers this spring. In a recent study at Kansas State University, women who kept brightly colored flowers in their workspaces were less stressed than women who kept a green foliage-type plant without flowers. The reason: Brightly colored flowers not only brighten the room but can capture our attention as well as give a quick mental break from negativity.
- What better time than Mother's Day to undertake an

indoor painting project? You've got warm weather, a captive workforce (they can't say no on your day), and a whole weekend to get it done.

HOMEkeeping and Organization

- Mother's Day signals the start of warm weather, so even if you choose to do not a whit of homekeeping or organization on your special day, use it as a starting point to attend to outdoor maintenance. Walk around the entire exterior of your home and grounds and make a list of everything that needs to be done.
- Consider renting or borrowing a power washer to clean the outside of your house, porch, and deck. Power washers have several different attachments for cleaning all types of surfaces.
- Spend a sunny May Saturday or Sunday scraping, priming, and painting peeling spots on trim or woodwork. You will protect the wood from the summer sun and prevent a costlier and more difficult job in the fall.
- Devote a day to cleaning and repairing screens for the upcoming open windows. Remove all screens from windows. To repair large holes, buy replacement screening at the hardware store. Smaller holes can be patched with small cutout pieces of screen. Tiny holes can be filled in with clear nail polish to keep bugs out. After repair, wash screens with warm, soapy water out on the back deck or in the yard. Rinse with the hose and

allow to air-dry. Consider spraying screens with bug repellent or Avon Skin-So-Soft before replacing screens in windows.

- Clean, inspect, and repair outdoor furniture. Flush gutters and downspouts with your hose. Wash and repaint your mailbox. Paint on a few flowers to liven it up.

- Mother's Day marks the end of flowering-bulb season. Deadhead daffodils, hyacinths, and tulips as the flowers wither and dry. Wait six weeks before mowing grass in areas where bulbs have naturalized.

- After Mother's Day, pinch back seedlings of marigolds, cosmos, and zinnias to coax branching out. Fertilize if

READER TO READER: CRAFT

Pick up some small terra-cotta flowerpots at a retail store. Along with the pots, buy some pastel-colored paints and a lettered stencil sheet. Have the kids help you paint the flowerpots pretty pastel colors. When the paint is dry, use your stencil sheet and white paint to imprint words such as "believe," "dream," "wish," "hope," or "love" on the flowerpots. Use these pretty and colorful flowerpots to brighten areas of your home. If the kids help, be sure to let them choose a flowerpot to brighten their room.

—Kim L., Cape Coral, Florida

leaves are yellowing. A milk-tea fertilizer can be prepared using a spadeful of manure in a cheesecloth-type tea bag steeped overnight in a bucket of water.

- Place stakes or growing rings around top-heavy, tall flowers (such as peonies and veronicas) before they reach half their height or they will flop.

Family

- Exercise your Mother's Day prerogative and get the kids involved in planting a family herb garden this year. Let each member of your family pick one herb to grow—mint, parsley, rosemary, thyme, tarragon are just some of the possibilities. If you don't have the room for a fresh herb garden in your yard, consider planting a container herb garden for the back deck or even kitchen.
- Stay connected to your own mother all year long. Resolve to surprise her with occasional bouquets of flowers and cards proclaiming your gratitude for her guidance.

FUN FACTS: MOTHER'S DAY

Sixty-three percent of moms keep all their Mother's Day cards. Each year, 136 million Mother's Day cards are sent.

- Spend a few minutes with each of your children looking through their baby books. Tell them how much you love being their mom!
- Start a mom's memory box for each of your children. Ask each of your children to draw a picture of you—be sure to put their name and age on the back and put these special pictures into your memory box. Making this an annual ritual will help you save precious memories.

Self

- Designate a spot in your garden or yard as "Mom's retreat." A chair or bench placed among flower beds or beside a shade tree makes a peaceful place to take a breather.
- Spend at least half an hour on Mother's Day in complete solitude. Make a list of all the things you've accomplished this year with and for your family. Anytime you need a little boost of energy, read through the list and glow with pride.
- Remind yourself that moms have needs, too, and giving too much of yourself away isn't good for anyone. Come up with at least three ways in which you can balance your needs with those of your family.
- Keep Mom healthy and schedule your annual appointment with your ob-gyn. If you're over forty, this is a good time to schedule your annual mammogram. If you're not, use today to do an extra-thorough breast self-exam.

- Treat yourself to a manicure this Mother's Day. Either head to a nail salon or do one at home. Soak your nails in lemon juice to cure everything from discolored nails to cracked cuticles. Lemons are a great source of alpha hydroxy acid, which exfoliates and softens cuticles without drying out nails.
- Seek out a sassy new haircut and/or color. Get rid of the dull winter split ends and bring on healthy, shining hair.

Grace Notes for May . . .

Memorial Day is among the few holidays that began as a "grassroots" observance. Beginning in the wake of the Civil War, communities across the United States were decorating the graves of their war dead. By the end of the nineteenth century, Memorial Day was being celebrated on May 30 throughout the country. It became official in 1971, when Congress declared the final Monday in May a national holiday.

Health

Tonight, re-create a healthy version of a favorite family recipe.

Fitness

March in your local parade, or in keeping with a holiday that honors the past, try out a few good old-fashioned games.

Hula hoop, leapfrog, Red Rover, hopscotch, even Duck, Duck, Goose—all burn more calories than playing Nintendo!

Home

Fly your United States flag at half-staff today until noon. Fly a POW/MIA flag today to honor prisoners of war and those missing in action.

Family

Visit the graves of your family and leave flowers.

Self

Pause to think about the true meaning of Memorial Day. Say a prayer for the men and women in wars. Spend some quiet time enjoying the memory of your own lost loved ones.

Cinco de Mayo

The fifth of May is not the anniversary of
Mexican independence, but rather a celebration
commemorating the battle of Puebla. On
May 5, 1862, a greatly outnumbered Mexican army
defeated the forces of the French, who were
looking to install a colonial government in Mexico City.
Although the French eventually succeeded,
their control over Mexico was short-lived,
and the celebration of Cinco de Mayo has endured
as a popular festival.

Health

Mexican food need not be fattening—there *are* healthy, delicious meals to be had south of the border! Tonight, whether
at home or at your favorite cantina, dine on fajitas. Stir-fry
onions, green peppers, and strips of chicken breast and
serve over soft whole-wheat tortillas. Top with salsa and fat-
free sour cream or plain yogurt. Serve with a side of beans
for extra fiber.

Fitness

Cinco de Mayo is a day for dancing! Crank up the mariachi music, grab your maracas, and shimmy and shake your way to a svelte new you.

Home

Hang a homemade piñata! Decorate a brown paper bag. Fill with fortunes, yo-yos, beaded necklaces, or small toys and trinkets, seal the opening with ribbons, and hang from a doorway. After dinner, take turns trying to hit the bag open with a broomstick while blindfolded!

Family

Dress the kids in brightly colored clothes today, a Mexican tradition.

Self

Unwind today. Sip a cold margarita and put your feet up!

June

Father's Day

Thanks to the efforts of a Washington woman
who had been raised by her widowed father, the
first Father's Day was observed on June 19, 1910,
in Spokane, Washington. In 1966 President
Lyndon Johnson signed a proclamation declaring
the third Sunday of June an official holiday.

Health

- Serve the man in your life breakfast in bed today—and go
  heavy on the fruit. According to Harvard Medical
  School, a diet rich in fruit and vegetables may help
  prevent prostate cancer. Don't forget to include the
  morning newspaper.
- Keep salmonella and other nasty little organisms at bay
  for your Father's Day barbecue. Cut raw meats on one
  cutting board and vegetables and fruits on another.
  Marinate meats and fish on the bottom shelf of your
  refrigerator and not on your kitchen counter. Boil the
  marinade for at least three minutes if you are planning
  to use it to baste your foods, and have a separate cooked-
  meat platter to serve your guests.

- If your guy is a confirmed carnivore, make it a point to be sure his meats are nitrite free. Nitrites, which are a preservative in some processed meats, are associated with high blood pressure and the risk of type 2 diabetes.
- Ask your husband to join you in your quest to eat a healthier, more balanced diet. Discuss better food choices, and how you can help each other to make them. Today of all days he should realize how important it is that he live a long, healthy life. Looking across the picnic table at his children should be incentive enough.
- This Father's Day, take a tip from those manliest of men, bodybuilders. They realized long ago that people who eat six smaller meals each day have lower body fat and more lean muscle than people who eat two to three times a day. Eating three smaller main meals and three healthy snacks can keep your body fueled and raise your metabolism level, which will give you more energy throughout the day. Snack on high-fiber and protein foods to keep your body engine revving.
- Serve iced tea instead of soda at your barbecue, and keep a pitcher of it in the fridge all summer long. You'll get disease-fighting antioxidants and flavonoids galore—all for absolutely zero calories.

**SIMPLE SUGGESTIONS FOR
CELEBRATORY MEALS**

To celebrate Father's Day in manly style, grill up some hearty meat and potatoes. Serve marinated grilled steak, grilled tuna, or grilled chicken. For a side, choose a variation on the versatile potato: roasted, baked, grilled, or cut into strips and baked into "fries." Accompany with an assortment of his favorite grilled veggies, including red, yellow, and green peppers, red onions, and portobello mushrooms. And for dessert, what better way to end this Father's Day meal but with an ice-cream sundae or root-beer float?

Fitness

- Grab your honey and do something unforgettably adventurous. Go rock climbing! Most states have indoor rock-climbing studios, which are perfect for first-timers. You'll learn how to tie the proper knots, spot each other safely, how to climb up, and how to rappel down. Climbing is great all-over exercise for you and your family.
- This Father's Day, help to keep your fella healthy by exercising together. If your spouse isn't inclined to work out on his own, ask him to be your fitness partner.
- Don your tennis whites and challenge your husband to a game of tennis today. Or team up to trounce some friends in a doubles tournament.

- Have a backyard relay race! Who really is faster, Mom or Dad?

FITNESS FOCUS: SHOULDERS
Strong shoulders aren't just for dads. There's nothing like shapely shoulders to set off a summer dress. This month, make it a point to try the following:

- Shoulder press: holding two five-pound dumbbells at ear level, press your arms straight up overhead. The weights should not touch above your head. Do two sets of eight to twelve.
- Side lifts: Standing with your feet hip distance apart, grasp your weights with your arms at your sides and palms facing down. Keeping a slight bend in your elbow, slowly lift your arms out to your sides until your hands are shoulder height, hold for one count, then lower weights slowly to start position. Do two sets of eight to twelve.
- Front lifts: Essentially the same as the side lift, but

FUN FACTS: FATHER'S DAY

- Eighty percent of Americans celebrate Father's Day.
- Fifty percent of all Father's Day cards are bought by children for their dads.
- $113 is the average amount spent on a Father's Day gift.

instead of raising your hands out to the side, raise your hands to shoulder height in front of you. You should feel the muscles in your shoulders working.

HOME Décor

- Have your kids help you plant a tree for their daddy. Consider planting a tree in memory of your or your husband's father or grandfather.
- Give a gift of joy. Think about artwork instead of the traditional Father's Day presents. Be sure to choose an image for your husband or father that you know he'll love. If it's for your husband, make certain you like it too—perhaps a piece that symbolizes romance for your bedroom.
- Give Dad a break from yardwork and recruit the kids to get the lawn looking beautiful for your Father's Day picnic.
- June is the perfect time of year to add some color to your home. The smallest of changes may brighten up your living spaces and keep you smiling all summer long. Choose bright throw pillows for your couch, add matching accessories like vases or area rugs, or paint a single wall of your home in a lovely shade that complements your décor.
- Invite the full spectrum of color indoors by hanging a crystal ball in your window. You'll have rainbows dancing on your walls and ceiling in no time!

> **CHITCHAT**
>
> When we moved to our home, my husband and I decided that we would create a hummingbird and butterfly garden. We filled it with a variety of red flowers that are a favorite of hummingbirds and a colorful array of flowering bushes and plants that appeal to butterflies. We added a birdbath for the birds and wind chimes for their lovely song. My son, who is fascinated with all of these wonderful creatures (especially the hummingbirds), now watches the garden and comes running for us to come and see them whenever they arrive.
>
> —Linda McClintock

HOMEkeeping and Organization

- For a great Father's Day treat, wash and clean out your husband's car. To make sure it smells as good as it looks, place a bowl of vinegar on the floor of the car the night before Father's Day and let it sit overnight. Vinegar absorbs odors that have seeped into rugs and upholstery so his car will be left smelling fresh.
- Spare Dad some hassle and clean the grill. Either clean it immediately after you've cooked, or turn the grill on and off for five to ten minutes before you begin. The heat will help the burned, caked-on food loosen up, and you should have no trouble scraping off what's left with a

stiff grill brush. If you don't have a grill brush, use a wad of crumpled aluminum foil to clean; just be careful not to burn yourself.

- You'll be popping in and out of the house during your picnic (and for the rest of the summer), so be sure your entryways are in order. Make sure your welcome mat does its job by keeping it clean. Get rid of spiderwebs, beehives, and everyday-living fingerprints and rain marks. If you have a sliding glass door to your backyard or patio, be sure the glass is clean and your screen doors are free of holes to keep the bugs out of your house. Put a sticker or sun catcher on the glass door so people won't inadvertently walk right into it.

- Whether you're on a Dad's Day camping expedition or just working in the yard, bug season has begun, so wear insect repellant to ward off mosquitoes and ticks. If you choose to use a repellent containing the powerful pesticide deet, use it sparingly, and try to spray it on clothing and not skin. (Note that deet reduces the effectiveness of sunblock by 30 percent. Children under six months should not use deet products at all, kids shouldn't use products with more than 10 percent deet, and adults shouldn't use a repellent with more than 30 percent deet.)

- Warm weather means it's time to wash your family pet(s). Why not give it a go after washing Dad's car? Chances are, you're already wet. Use a shampoo for your animal's type (dry, flaky skin; normal; or oily), and after his bath, let him dry off in the sun. He will love you for it, and it will be fun for the whole family. Take this opportunity to clean out your pet's living and sleeping quarters.

Family

- Let your hubby have a full eighteen-hole day of golf today with his buddies . . . no complaints! The Dad's Day picnic dinner can wait till he gets back.
- If your guy is the outdoor type, go camping this weekend. Bring a stargazing book and pick out the constellations and planets. Have a contest to see who can catch the most fireflies; the winner can tell the first spooky story of the night.
- Take a photo of your kids, and then have them decorate a Father's Day frame. What could be nicer for Dad's desk at work than a picture of his progeny?
- Spend Father's Day afternoon bowling with the kids, then head out to the restaurant of Dad's choice for a special Father's Day lunch.
- Haul out the hammer, nails, and a few pieces of wood and spend Father's Day afternoon building birdhouses. These one-of-a-kind creations will always remind Dad of his special day for years to come.
- Go fishing! Pack up a picnic lunch and all Dad's bait and tackle. Spend a relaxing afternoon fishing and enjoying one another's company.
- Ask your young children to answer questions about their father or grandfather. How old is he? What kind of car

does he drive? How much does he weigh? Where does he work? What is his favorite hobby or sport? Write down their answers, date them, and present them to Dad in a small memory box.

- Crown Daddy "king for the day." Earlier in the week, assist the children and construct a paper crown for him to wear. Let him choose his favorite meal for dinner, and let him rule the remote control tonight!

Self

- Use today as an opportunity to connect with your own father. If your dad is the old-fashioned sort and ill-accustomed to talking about feelings, why not write him a note? If he's since passed away, take some time to flip through an old photo album and write down a treasured memory.
- Summer's here! Treat your feet and your partner's feet to a pedicure. During your footbath, gently exfoliate your feet with a scrub (either one purchased at your local pharmacy or a homemade paste of 1 cup of sugar and ½ cup extra-virgin olive oil), rinse, then rub a pumice stone around the edges of your feet, especially where the calluses are. Pat dry and apply a heavy moisturizer or a special foot cream, pull on cotton socks, and wear them to bed for baby-soft feet come morning.
- Not just moms love massages—dads dig them too! Tonight, trade back rubs with your spouse. Use a good-quality,

unrefined oil (like almond oil, avocado oil, grape-seed oil, or safflower oil, etc.), add a few drops of orange, ginger, tea tree, rosemary, lemongrass, or lavender oil, and massage away aches and pains. Place the oil in a heatproof glass and place in a bowl of hot water to warm the oil up.

- Now that warmer weather is here, take a few minutes a couple times a week to steam your face. Steaming your face opens pores and clears out any oily buildup. Simply fill the sink with hot water, cover your head with a towel, and lean close to the steaming water for two or three minutes.

- Father's Day marks the beginning of bathing suit season. Try to shop early in the day, when you will be less bloated. Even if you don't think a suit will be flattering, try it on; it may surprise you. Consider tops and bottoms that are sold separately; dark to minimize and light or bright to highlight a certain area. There is a suit for you; you just need to find it. And the right suit for you will be a gift for your husband, too.

Grace Notes
for June . . .

Graduation Celebrations

**A time to celebrate this academic milestone of
our student scholars . . . young and old!**

Health

Watch out for emotional eating on graduation day. Before
you reach for that tasty little snack, ask yourself, "Am I hungry?" or are you eating because you feel anxious, sad, happy,
or ambivalent that your little one is not so little anymore?
Most folks who overeat do so as a result of emotional triggers; count on today being *full* of them, and try to think
through the impulse to eat.

Fitness

Set up a badminton net in your yard and challenge kids to a
game. Create teams according to class years—1986 versus

2006. Or wrap a piece of paper around a dowel to look like a diploma, secure with a ribbon, and have a graduation-themed relay race.

Home

Decorate your home in the school colors of the graduate you are honoring, using the same colors for the paper goods, balloons, and flowers.

Family

Present a congratulatory toast to the graduate at the celebration tonight. Come armed with several of his childhood school photos!

Self

Deep belly-breathing helps to calm nerves. Remember, this is a new start for you and your graduate, *not* an ending.

The Wedding Anniversary

A day to honor husbands and wives
and their union together.

Health

Skip the restaurant dessert and come home to celebrate.
Feature a low-fat trifle for a healthy treat the whole family
will enjoy. Layer a glass trifle dish with angel food cake
pieces, fat-free yogurt, fruits of choice, and a low-fat
whipped topping!

Fitness

Dance to your wedding song with your spouse.

Home

Set a sweet and celebratory breakfast table. In the center, place your lit wedding candle, and nearby, a handmade "Happy Anniversary" sign. Sprinkle heart-shaped confetti around the coffee cups, and serve heart-shaped pancakes or toast. Surprise your spouse when he steps out of the shower with "Happy Anniversary" written on the mirror with soap, or if you're daring, red lipstick!

Family

Add to your wedding anniversary album. On each page, mount a photo of you and your spouse. If you are starting a new album, use your anniversary week to sort through your photo boxes and albums and select one photo for each anniversary year past. And be sure to add new ones annually in the years to come.

Self

Snuggle up with your spouse, watch your wedding video or flip through your wedding album, and reminisce. Pop some champagne and enjoy!

July

Independence Day

Each year on July 4, America celebrates
Independence Day, the anniversary of the
signing of the Declaration of Independence
in 1776, when colonists declared their
freedom from British rule.

Health

- July Fourth marks the start of berry season. At peak
  right now are strawberries, raspberries, and fresh
  currants, which are great for pies and jams. By month's
  end, blueberries will also be in abundance. Be sure to
  put berries on the finger food menu for your July Fourth
  picnic.
- Keep folks grazing with a hearty assortment of crudités.
  Vegetables are high in fiber, which fills you up, low in
  simple sugars, low in calories, and high in
  phytochemicals that boost your overall immunity.
- Prepare an easy, low-cal sauce that's yummy over fish or
  as a dip for vegetables. Simply combine ⅔ cup nonfat

READER TO READER

Trading carbs and replacing bad fats with good fats were two steps I never thought I'd be able to accomplish until I came up with an easy solution. Instead of counting calories and dissecting food labels every day I simply count fruits and veggies now. I get at least five a day, but when I want to lose some weight, I aim for more. This fills me up and keeps me on the right track effortlessly.

—Marjorie D., Freeport, Maine

---

plain yogurt, ½ cup diced cucumber (seeds removed), and 3 tbs. chopped fresh dill. Enjoy!
- Scatter little bowls of dried fruits for easy nibbling. Packed with potassium, antioxidants, and fiber, they make a healthy snack for everyone.

FUN FACTS: INDEPENDENCE DAY

More than 67 million Americans cook on their grills on the Fourth of July, making it the most popular holiday for home barbecuing (followed by Memorial Day and Labor Day). A whopping 90 percent of Americans would opt for a meal from the grill over a five-course dinner, according to the thirteenth annual Weber Grillwatch Survey.

- Serve a tray of lightly salted whole-wheat rice cakes in lieu of potato chips. Garnish with a few sliced fresh tomatoes for a colorful combo!
- Be careful not to sabotage your healthy diet with condiments. Using mustard instead of mayo on your turkey burger will save you about 180 calories and 20 grams of fat.
- Save some time and don't preshuck your corn on the cob. Grilling corn in its silk leaf casing will help it to retain flavor and moisture. Pile the ears high on a tray to keep them warm longer.
- If you're hosting a large get-together for friends, kick off your celebration with an easy and festive tray full of mimosas! Place a fresh strawberry in a champagne glass (plastic ones will work fine for backyards); top with fresh squeezed orange juice and a splash of champagne.

CRAFT BOX:
CORK-LINED SERVING TRAY

An easy-to-make cork-lined serving tray will come in handy when serving the lemonade or mimosas by preventing glasses from sliding. Purchase a roll of $1/8$-inch thick cork sheet (available at most craft or home hardware supply stores). Trace the bottom of a tray or metal cookie sheet onto a piece of cork and cut it out with scissors. Affix the cork inside the tray with double-sided tape.

Consider making mimosas your "featured drink," and then serving sparkling waters, lemonade, beer, and wine for a workable—but not overwhelming—bar that will please everyone.

- Place your salad plates in the fridge before the party begins to keep produce crisper and cooler when it's time to serve.
- Place balsamic vinegar into a clean glass spray bottle so guests can spritz as much or as little as desired onto their salads, veggie kebabs, or burgers.
- If you live in an apartment or condo or opt not to turn on an outdoor grill, chicken salad served in whole-wheat flour tortillas or on crisp beds of romaine lettuce makes an easy and healthful alternative.

SIMPLE SUGGESTIONS FOR CELEBRATORY MEALS

Because the United States is so diverse, there are plenty of traditional foods to choose from for your Independence Day picnic. In the Northeastern part of the States, a Fourth of July picnic might include Boston baked beans, crab cakes, steamed lobster, corn chowder, and coleslaw. Down south, traditional July Fourth meals include barbecued shrimp, stewed okra, black-eyed peas, corn bread, fried green tomatoes, jerk pork sandwiches, and southern-fried chicken, followed by coconut cake or chocolate-bourbon-pecan cake. Midwestern favorites include hot dogs, hamburgers, corn on the cob, macaroni salad, watermelon, and apple pie. In the Southwest, where the food can be hotter than the fireworks, an Independence Day feast might include glazed ribs, fajitas, fish tacos with guacamole, and for dessert, coconut ice cream, margarita cheesecake, or coconut flan. Pacific Northwest favorites include sesame-crusted seared salmon; boiled Dungeness crab; caramelized onion, gorgonzola, and rosemary pizza; deep-dish mixed-berry pie, strawberry ice-cream soda; and chai milk shakes.

Fitness

- Take your daily walk today in the cool early-morning hours. If you wait till later, you'll be cutting into your picnic-planning time and competing with the midday heat.
- Get into the spirit of Independence Day by incorporating an old-fashioned tug-of-war into your backyard picnic festivities. Tie several big knots to use as handles on either end of a very thick rope and divide your party guests into two teams. Think "Stars" versus "Stripes" or "Blue" against "Red." Tug away and see which team has been working out!
- Before your guests arrive, put a fitness ball on a beach blanket in the middle of your yard; then watch how many people are drawn to it—whether to exercise, experiment, or just fool around. If you're looking to buy a ball, bear the following in mind: Your knees and hips should be at the same height when you sit on it. If you're less than five feet tall, opt for a 45-centimeter ball; if

you're between five and six feet, try one that's 55 centimeters; and if you are over six feet tall, go with a 65-centimeter model. Bigger balls may be more expensive or harder to find, but working with a too-small ball can overstress your back. The bigger the ball, the more support it offers.

- July Fourth marks the start of swim season. This month, when you are at the beach, at a lake, or in a pool, use the water to work out. Although water is eight hundred times denser than air, water exercise causes no stress to joints and can burn between 300 and 500 calories an hour.

FITNESS FOCUS: LEGS

Bear in mind that water exercise is a particularly handy method for working legs because it's easy on injury-prone knees and ankles.

- Standing in chest-deep water and holding on to the side of the pool with both hands, keep one leg straight and kick it out behind you (as if you are doing a battement in ballet). Do eight to twenty-five reps, then switch legs.
- While neck-deep in water, "cross-country ski." Swing your arms and legs in opposition, working against the natural resistance of the water. See if you can keep going—and keep your head above water—for five full minutes.
- Straddle a Styrofoam water noodle as if you were riding a bicycle. Start "pedaling" with your legs and try to maintain for a full five minutes.

HOME Décor

- Think simple, sweet, and rustic for your July Fourth picnic. Cover your picnic table with a red-and-white gingham cloth and display a crawling vine of fresh tomatoes as a "runner." Use red, white, and blue paper goods and plastic ware. Bright buckets filled with fresh daisies make easy, no-fuss centerpieces.

- The day before you entertain, visit your local copy shop and make photocopies of the lyrics to "The Star-Spangled Banner." Roll each sheet like an old-fashioned mail scroll, tie with red and blue ribbons, and put one at every place setting. Starting or ending the meal with a group song will liven things up!

- Set up your boom box or portable radio in the backyard for your picnic music. Keep a small basket of CDs and tapes beside it with a note welcoming all guests to play the music of their choice today.

- If your picnic will stretch into the evening, scatter small mason jars with votive candles throughout your backyard (on rocks in the flower garden, tied to trees, or on all the picnic tables).

- Place a fresh or frozen raspberry in each section of an ice cube tray, fill with water, and freeze the night before. You'll have healthy and beautiful fruit-splashed ice cubes to serve with your drinks. How festive to serve them in a clear glass ice bucket!

- Tend to your flower garden the morning of your picnic or the day before to make sure the weeds have been pulled and it looks its summer best. Practice deadheading your potted plants every day through the summer months. Be sure to water the lawn and all your gardens in the early morning or late afternoon.

- If you have a pool party planned for the Fourth of July, be sure to prop a few small flags into flowerpots around the pool and have plenty of red, white, and blue beach towels folded and ready for the guests.

- Fill a large glass flower vase with whole lemons, limes, and oranges and insert slices of each on the outer edge showing through the vase. Fill with water and display pretty fresh-cut flowers for a buffet table or bar centerpiece.

- For additional backyard seating, pull out an old trunk and place a colorful (or red-white-and-blue) cushion on it.

HOMEkeeping and Organization

- The night before Independence Day, get your thermos containers rinsed out and ready to go, along with your picnic basket supplies. If you're headed to someone else's holiday celebration, pack a big wicker picnic basket with additional healthy family snacks (especially if you have finicky eaters), your hostess gift, camera, wine, or anything else to be carried to the picnic and, more important, taken back home.

- If you are traveling with younger children to a celebration with evening fireworks, be sure to pack a

CHITCHAT

A great way to organize photos is to create separate albums devoted to a particular holiday. I started with my big Christmas scrapbook, then began my medium sized Easter album, another for Halloween, and just a few years ago I decided to start a small Fourth of July photo album. I painted an American flag on the blue fabric cover of a small album, and then added a few photos of my family at our beach-house parties with each year printed boldly on the pages. It has become such a joy to flip through sunny photos of children splashing by the beach, snapshots of my sister and friends in their sporty sunglasses, and photos of sparklers lighting up the flag cake. My Fourth of July album gets displayed on our coffee table the first of July and makes a delightful conversation piece and heirloom!

—Lisa Lelas

small bag with the kids' pajamas (a sweatshirt too, if the weather calls for it). It makes the return trip home a bit easier for you when the kids can get right to bed.

• If you're hosting a big backyard party, consider splurging and renting tables, chairs, and linens. It will make the barbecue look and feel special and will provide more comfort to your guests. The best part, however, is when the rental company comes to pick up the furniture and linens for an easy cleanup!

- Use laundry baskets for quick prepicnic housecleaning. With each room you are about to clean, line up five small laundry baskets, bins, or boxes. Label each with the following: "Garbage," "Hang up or put away," "Belongs in another part of the house," "Laundry," and "Give Away." Begin cleaning by picking up clutter and tossing each item into the appropriate basket.
- If traveling for a long weekend getaway this July Fourth, make it a point to wash the inside of your car windshield today. And clean your sunglasses while you're at it.
- Don't let picnic stains get you down. To remove ketchup or barbecue sauce from fabric, flush or blot with water. Apply a few drops of mild white dishwashing liquid. Rinse. If needed, soak in white vinegar. Then launder the garment.
- Summer water sports are delightful, but less fun is the mildewed laundry that so often attends them. Badly mildewed items, such as wet beach towels your child left hidden in the garage, may be damaged beyond repair. Sunlight can sometimes help by killing the fungus. If the garment is bleach-safe, soak for up to fifteen minutes in a mild solution of 1 ounce chlorine bleach to 1 gallon cool water. Rinse with ¼ cup white household vinegar diluted in 1 gallon water, then rinse again with plain water. Launder as usual.

Family

- Even if you don't want to entertain a crowd, have a family picnic today. Check your local newspaper for parades or evening fireworks celebrations and plan an outing.
- Take your kids to the market with you. Getting your kids involved with shopping for the July Fourth barbecue will not only get them excited about helping at the picnic but, because they were a part of the food selection process, may actually get them to eat the meal!

FUN FACTS: INDEPENDENCE DAY

According to one theory, fireworks originated in China a thousand years ago, when a cook who was experimenting with fuels ignited a volatile mixture of sulfur, charcoal, and saltpeter.

- Cherish the warm summer evenings surrounding the Fourth of July by taking your children out to the backyard to look for fireflies. As you do, make up a story together. Perhaps you'll pretend the lightning bugs are fairies holding lanterns to light their way, or maybe glowing princesses in a magical world. Whatever you and your children decide, make this an opportunity to exercise your imaginations.

- Don't wait until your child says she's thirsty to give her something to drink. By then she's already dehydrated. Equip your kids with water/sports bottles labeled with their names and encourage them to keep sipping throughout the day.
- Beat summer boredom by taking a cue from our Victorian forebears: suggest to your children that they begin any winter holiday gift creations this month. Resourceful Victorian mothers instituted "Christmas in July" celebrations and used the summers to knit, sew, or craft holiday gifts so that they were free to do other holiday planning come fall.
- Prepare the family pets for the loud fireworks tonight. If you have a dog with a tendency to get overexcited or nervous, consider creating a quiet place for him in a back room or basement with his food, water, and bed. If you have a pet that typically shakes with fear from loud noises, you may want to take him to your vet.
- Be a kid with your kids! Run through a backyard sprinkler with your children today . . . do it again when the guests arrive!
- Keep kids in the academic habit by inviting a handful of friends and neighbors for a parent-child "Summer Book Club and Barbecue." If all the kids are around the same age, assign the same book to everyone; if you've got a mix of ages and reading levels, let each child choose his book, then take turns at the party describing what it was about. It's a great way to get your kids excited about reading.

Self

- Visit a park and boost your willpower this Fourth of July season. Research shows that people who regularly spend time in parks, in the woods—or anyplace where they are exposed to nature—improve their ability to concentrate, stay calm during confrontations, and pass up unhealthy snacks.

- Like it or not, July Fourth means swimsuit season, and swimsuit season means shaving. Time to smooth up and "bare" down for the beach. Make shaving easier by waiting three minutes in the shower for the water to soften your hair. Use shaving gels rather than shaving creams, which can be drying, and be sure to change your razor blade at the first sign of dullness (usually after three or four shaves).

- Before July 4, make sure you purchase a pair of water shoes. You'll be more likely to take a swim if the sharp or slimy bottom surface is not an issue. Water shoes also protect your feet from cuts and abrasions and the bacteria that can creep in.

- Now's the time to pick up inexpensive trial sizes of sunscreens and antibacterial lotions. Throw a few of them in your glove compartment for unexpected visits to the park or beach on sunny summer days.

- The best way to get cool on a sweltering summer day is in your shower! According to the Spa de Soleil in Los Angeles, you should start off with warm water. After

three minutes, turn up the heat. When you are toasty,
reverse it back to lukewarm and then finish with a cool
blast. The changes of hot and cold on your body will
keep your skin cool for the next couple of hours.

- Heading to the beach? Boost your mood with this
supersimple refreshing step! Apply three to five drops
of your favorite essential oil, such as calming lavender,
on a clean, dry washcloth and toss it into the dryer with
a load of beach towels.

- Keep sweaty summer skin blemish free. Saturate a
cotton swab with lime or lemon juice and dab blemishes
before going to bed. The phytochemicals in citrus draw
out pore-clogging oils overnight, so you wake up with a
clearer complexion.

- Just look at lemons and feel better! Feasting your eyes
on lemons sets off a biochemical chain of events that
instantly lifts moods. The energy frequencies emitted by
the bright yellow actually alleviate sadness.

- Don't let the celebrations of the day distract you from
taking care of your skin. Pick sunscreen with an SPF of 15
or higher. Be sure it says "broad-spectrum" protection,
meaning it shields skin from two types of ultraviolet rays:
burning rays from the summer sun and the so-called aging
rays, which are prevalent year round. Apply sunscreen at
least fifteen minutes before you go outside, and wear a
brimmed hat for extra protection. Recently, the federal
Department of Health and Human Services added UV
radiation from the sun and artificial sources to its
comprehensive list of known carcinogens. Approximately
32 percent of Americans get sunburned each year!

Grace Notes
for July . . .

Family Reunions

A time to bring together extended family members
from around the country to introduce new generations,
reestablish lost connections, and renew old traditions.

Health

A few weeks before the reunion, request that all family
members contribute a favorite healthy recipe. Share them
on a Web site or have them bound and make this "family
cookbook" your gift to all the attendees.

Fitness

Hold sack races, relay races, and flag football games with the
various generations as different teams. Put up a scoreboard
(made of plywood and paint or poster board and markers) to
keep the challenge more exciting!

Home

As picnic table centerpieces, create arrangements of old family photos and framed baby pictures of the folks present. To promote mingling, place a playing card (using matching cards from two decks or more) at every place setting, and encourage both children and adults to use the afternoon to find out which family member has their matching card.

Family

Be sure to take a family photo. Have each branch of the family tree wear a particular color T-shirt.

Self

Nurture your soul with laughter today. Share a joke and encourage others to follow.

Bastille Day

On July 14, 1789, the people of Paris rose up and
stormed the Bastille, a notorious prison that symbolized
the absolute power of the monarchy that ruled France.
Like American Independence Day, Bastille Day
celebrates the beginning of the French Revolution, and
the founding of a government led by the people.

Health

Celebrate Bastille Day with a glass of red wine. Studies have
shown that drinking one glass a day of red wine is good for
your heart. Head to your local wine store and pick up a bottle
of merlot, cabernet, Bordeaux, Côtes du Rhône . . . the selection is *fantastique*!

Fitness

You need not be training for the Tour de France to enjoy the
excellent health benefits of bicycling. Plan a long bike ride—
add a few hills for a challenge—strap on your helmet and go!

Home

Pick up an inexpensive frame from your local discount store to display a postcard or print by your favorite French painter. Whether one of Claude Monet's images of the lush gardens of Giverny, Edgar Degas's elegant dancers, or Pierre-Auguste Renoir's adorable children, this is an almost effortless way to enrich your décor.

Family

Take the family to the ballet. Or, if your *famille* is less inclined to dance, take in a soccer game.

Self

Infuse some joie de vivre into your next shopping trip and buy yourself something French: a bottle of French perfume, a chic new scarf, or even a croissant and a café au lait.

August

Birthday Celebrations

Originally, only kings celebrated their birthdays.
The first known birthday celebrations for children
began in Germany and were called "kinderfests." Back
in the Victorian era, it is believed that birthdays became
big celebrations because, in a time when children's
mortality rates were 50 percent, families truly
had reason to celebrate that each child
had made it to another birthday.

Health

- If today is *your* birthday, make a special effort to eat
  sensibly. Don't use your birthday as an excuse to
  abandon your healthy lifestyle—and don't take a break
  from writing in your food journal. Did you know that the
  average woman gains nine pounds between her thirtieth
  and thirty-ninth birthdays, and the average man gains
  four?
- This year, on the morning of your child's birthday, make
  special pancakes in her honor. Add some wheat germ in
  the mix to make them fiber and protein rich. After the
  pancakes are cooked, use food coloring to write either
  the child's first initial or age in the pancakes. Top the

pancake stack with a candle and gather around the
breakfast table to sing "Happy Birthday."

- Let your kids make their own birthday lunch. Give each
child an individual-size ball of pizza dough (or a
premade crust like Boboli). Have the sauce and toppings
in small bowls on the table and let each child decorate
his or her own pizza. Encourage fun designs like a
smiley face made with two olives for eyes, a slice of red
pepper for the mouth, and a piece of pineapple for the
nose!

- Beware of serving fruit drinks to children at parties.
Unless the label states 100 percent fruit juice, many fruit
drinks are only 5 percent juice and loaded with sugar.
Likewise, avoid serving caffeinated drinks like soda and
iced tea. Caffeine is a diuretic, meaning it accelerates
water loss. Kids could become dehydrated and
light-headed after an afternoon of running around.
Instead, make water the featured drink. Children are
more apt to welcome H_2O if you keep a batch of
individual-size bottled waters on ice in a big red wagon!

- Ditch the traditional goody bag for a party favor that's
nicer, healthier, and easier on you! As guests leave, give
each child a wrapped game or toy with a "thank you for
coming to my party" note from your child. Whenever
you see a bargain buy at your favorite discount store
throughout the year, pick up several. Be sure to have the
birthday child hand out the party favors. This will
remind him/her to say "thank you" as well.

SHOWSTOPPER CUPCAKES FOR EVERY SEASON!

Winter snowman: On top of white icing, stack two marshmallows (one full-size on bottom, a smaller one on top; slice a piece off this marshmallow and squeeze it to make it even smaller). A dab of icing will hold them together. Place a chocolate-covered mint on top as the snowman's beret hat, cut a carrot-shaped nose from a gummy fish, and poke two small holes with a toothpick and insert two chocolate sprinkles for eyes!

Spring lollipop flowers: Cover a mound of white icing on each cupcake with sprinkles. Insert a lollipop (as the flower) and add a leaf cut from green Fruit Roll-Up at the base of the lollipop stem.

Summer beach party: Cover half of the cupcakes with white icing and roll in graham-cracker crumbs (for a beach-sand look) and top with a small paper cocktail parasol (as the beach umbrella). Top the other half of the cupcakes with blue icing and insert a blue triangle "wave" cut from blue construction paper.

Autumn apples: Top cupcakes with red icing. Insert a pretzel stick into each one (as the apple stem) and garnish with a green leaf cut from sour fruit tape.

SIMPLE SUGGESTIONS FOR
CELEBRATORY MEALS

This year, celebrate with dinner themes chosen by the birthday boy, girl, mom, or dad. Mexican fiesta dinners can include homemade guacamole, tacos, black beans, fresh salsa, and a pineapple angel food cake. For an Italian theme, feature assorted antipasti for starters, vegetable lasagna, pasta with meatballs, or a veal scaloppine with lemon and fennel, crusty whole-grain bread, a tossed salad, tomato-basil-mozzarella toss, and a rum cake. For a Japanese theme, serve boiled edamame (soybeans), miso soup, chicken or salmon teriyaki, rice, steamed broccoli, and green-tea ice cream for dessert. Don't forget the sake!

Fitness

- Make the next birthday party you throw a fun social experience wrapped around some sort of exercise . . . a volleyball birthday bash, a softball game, or a good ol' dance party.
- Have the birthday celebrant choose a fun family activity such as hiking, ice skating, Rollerblading, or bicycling. Spend some time the weekend before the party on this healthy family activity.
- Put sessions with a personal trainer on your birthday wish list. Or ask for a gift certificate to a yoga or Pilates studio.
- If you are hosting or attending a dinnertime birthday celebration, try to take a quick stroll at about four thirty

P.M. to avoid the afternoon urge to snack before dinner. That's the most common time that dieters cheat. Low energy and increased tension peak in the late afternoon, but taking a brisk walk for even five minutes can cut in half the desire to eat, according to Robert Thayer, Ph.D., California State University at Long Beach.

FITNESS FOCUS: FLEXIBILITY

As you get older, you lose flexibility—particularly in your lower back—so make it this month's goal to incorporate stretches into your daily routine. Some simple stretches include:

- Slowly roll your shoulders forward eight times, then back eight times. Gently incline your right ear toward your right shoulder—and slowly extend your left arm. You should feel a stretch across the side of your neck. Now do the other side.
- With feet a little more than hip distance apart, bend your knees into a partial squat and place your hands on the tops of your thighs. Gently round your back, contract your stomach muscles, tuck in your chin, and let your spine curve. Then, keeping your hands where they are, arch your back and stick your chin out. Repeat several times.
- Standing with feet shoulder width apart and your knees soft, bend forward and let your head and hands hang loosely toward the floor. Be sure to relax your neck—don't try to look up. You should feel a stretch up the back of your legs and across your lower back.

HOME Décor

• Here's a unique way to display pictures of the birthday boy: Place bendable action figures with their arms outstretched near the birthday cake and prop up photos of the birthday boy on their arms. Use Barbie dolls to hold up pics of your daughter!

CRAFT BOX:
EUROPEAN BIRTHDAY LIFE CANDLES

In Germany, where the custom of celebrating birthdays originally began, it is traditional to light a beautifully decorated life candle on a child's birthday. You can make your own life candle by purchasing a plain white tall and sturdy candle (approximately 12 inches or 30 centimeters tall). Measure the candle with a ruler and place marks every inch going down the candle. Using sequin pins, place sequins at every inch mark. Each mark will indicate a birth year, so with a marker write a number next to the sequins, starting with 1 at the top and continuing through 12 at the bottom. Decorate the rest of the candle with wax candle stickers, available at craft shops. The birthday child should burn the candle on his birthday until the line reaches the next birth number. Store the candle to use again next year.

- Jazz up a birthday cake without spending a fortune. Add a little more color and sweetness to your child's cake with edible candleholders made out of fruit-flavored Life Savers on top. Pop in the candles and make a wish!
- Creative lighting will enhance any party atmosphere. Replace some of your regular lightbulbs with colored bulbs. Or if you want to be more elaborate, string twinkle lights in trees, or hang Japanese paper lanterns.
- Start a birthday tablecloth this year. Each year either paint or trace the birthday child's hand- and footprint on the tablecloth. Write the year and age below the print.

FUN FACTS: BIRTHDAY TRADITIONS FROM AROUND THE WORLD

- Brazil/Italy—The birthday child receives a pull on the earlobe for each year he has been alive.
- Canada—The birthday child is ambushed and her nose is greased with butter or margarine for good luck. The grease makes the child too slippery for bad luck to catch her.
- China—Long noodles are served to wish the birthday child a long life.
- England—Foil-covered coins are dropped into the cake batter and baked inside. If you get a coin in your piece of cake, you will become rich.

Display the tablecloth each year during the child's birthday week and consider having guests sign it!

- On the night before his birthday, after your little one is asleep, hang colorful streamers in front of his door. When he awakens, he'll begin the day in a festive, special way. Or fill your child's closet with helium balloons in her favorite colors. On her birthday morning, when she opens the closet to get dressed, she'll be greeted with a burst of excitement.

HOMEkeeping and Organization

- Limit the mess by containing the party to a particular area of your home. Hang cute and funny "Off-limits" signs on rooms you don't want kids wandering into.

READER TO READER

After birthday celebrations, I like to use thank-you notes as bookmarks in my cookbooks. It's a welcome surprise to look up a recipe and reminisce over a note . . . some of which are now more than twenty years old!

—Barbara B., Madison, Connecticut

- Buy the birthday girl or boy a new pillow for his or her bed. Bed pillows need to be changed every year, and birthdays are a great reminder.

- Be inventive during your postparty cleanup. Run scraps of wrapping paper through a paper shredder and store them in a small drawstring bag. Use the shreds for confetti and in place of tissue paper in gift bags.
- If your child's birthday coincides with a major holiday, consider choosing another time of year to celebrate. Lesley Ingves-Hooke of Functionality Professional Organizing says that since her own and her daughter's birthdays fall so close to Christmas, they both began celebrating their half-birthdays at the end of June. Lesley gives her daughter a small gift on her actual birth

---

FUN FACT: BIRTHDAYS

Did you know that in China many people do not celebrate on the day they were born? Instead, each winter, during Chinese New Year, every Chinese person turns a year older together no matter when his or her real birthday falls! Many Chinese people believe that a baby is one year old when it's born (his first *birth* day!). A Chinese child's second birthday (which would be your first) is celebrated by having the child find its own fortune. Parents put the toddler in front of various objects and watch to see which one he will grab first. A baby who grabs a coin might become rich; a baby who reaches for a book might become a writer or teacher; a baby who grabs a doll might have many children, etc.

date, then reminds her of the party to come that won't get buried in the holiday rush.

Family

- Remember that the focus of the birthday is the person celebrating, not the party you're throwing. Why not give a modest party the weekend before or after the birthday? Then on the birthday celebrant's actual day of birth, have an intimate party at home with close family.
- If you're planning a party for a child, be sure to involve him or her in the party planning and preparation. It's fun and exciting for children to pick a theme, location,

---

READER TO READER

I simplified much of my life using tips from the Simple Steps program. I went back to the basics with so many things, including birthday parties. We now invite the number of guests that matches the birthday child's age. At my son's fifth birthday party, we had five of his friends over to celebrate. My daughter turns seven this year and she is already choosing her guest list of seven! It has been so much easier than hosting a houseful of classmates!

—Sharon L., Madison, Wisconsin

guest list, games, and type of cake. Have them help you make the appetizers, decorate, and straighten up the house before guests arrive.

- On the eve of a young child's birthday, attach some glow-in-the-dark stars to her bedroom ceiling. Lie in bed and help her make wishes for the year ahead . . . and make it a part of your bedtime ritual every night thereafter.

- If your child's birthday falls on a school day, tuck a birthday card and cupcake into his lunch box. Or consider bringing or sending along a box full of festive cupcake "cones" to school that your child can share with her class. Half fill a flat-bottomed ice-cream cone with cake batter and bake as usual. (Cones should be standing up, of course.) Top cones with a favorite frosting and pack them together in a small cardboard box. Both teachers and students will appreciate the no-mess treats.

- For the next grown-up birthday party you throw, consider incorporating the theme of helping others into the celebration. On the invitation, in lieu of a gift, ask guests to bring a gently worn adult-size coat to be donated to a needy person. By the party's end, you'll be amazed at how many coats you've collected.

- Whether your child is turning one or ten, throw a book party and give the gift of reading! Ask each guest to bring a book as a birthday gift. It can be a fairy tale, an adult classic that your child can grow into, or a copy of that guest's favorite childhood story. Whatever the book,

---

CHITCHAT

Since they were newborns, both of my daughters have had their own guest books. Even at the hospital, I asked visitors coming to see the new baby to "sign in." I've displayed these books at each of their birthday celebrations thereafter, labeling the particular year ("Lexy's Pony Party—three years old," etc.) and asking guests to add a few words. Displaying the book alongside a big feather quill pen and an eight-by-ten framed photo of the birthday girl is such a joy!

—Lisa Lelas

---

make sure each of your guests inscribes it. What a wonderful way to build your child a library she can cherish forever!

- Consider having a "card shower" to celebrate the birthday of an elderly person you know. The invitation should read something like, "In honor of Marie Rizzo's eightieth birthday, we're having a card shower! We'd like family and friends to shower her with cards." For a shut-in or an older person who lives far away, imagine the joy she'll experience in opening a mailbox overflowing with good wishes!
- Videotape a quick interview with your child on his or her birthday, and, using the same tape every year, continue this tradition. Use some point of height reference as the

backdrop, such as a garden bench or the front door of your home.

- Start a one-photo-per-page birthday album for each person in your family. Each year, choose a head shot of your child (a snapshot is fine) and have it enlarged into an eight-by-ten. With a marker or adhesive number, simply record his or her age at the top corner of each page.

- The day after the party, help your child write thank-you notes. They are an important social-skill builder. Most kids actually enjoy writing thank-you cards, either by hand or on the computer. If your child is too young to

---

CHITCHAT

Every year on the eve of my daughters' birthdays, I write them each a letter telling them how much they are loved, how their birth has changed my life, how quickly they are growing up, and the accomplishments the past year has brought. My husband also adds his warm words to the letter, and then we sign it, kiss it, and seal it. I am keeping the birthday letters in a beautiful hat box in my master closet, which I plan to package with ribbons someday to present to them on their future wedding days!

—Lisa Lelas

write his own, have him dictate a note; then sign it and stuff the envelope.

· This year, on your special day, take a few minutes to write *your* mother and father a note, thanking them for a life worth celebrating.

Self

· Pamper yourself with an invigorating summer shower! The morning of your big party, slather on a paste made of equal parts fine yellow cornmeal and honey. Massage the mixture all over, but especially on knees, elbows, and heels, then rinse with *warm* water. You'll have softer, smoother, and younger-looking skin . . . no matter what birthday this is!

· If today is your birthday, light a candle and make a wish. Traditionally birthday candles were thought to have carried wishes up to God.

READER TO READER

My dad began a lovely tradition. On my birthday and each of my siblings' birthdays, Dad presents my Mom with a bouquet of roses. He honors her on our birthdays and thanks her with roses for the wonderful gift of his children.

—Maria L., New York, New York

- This birthday, resolve to stay fit not only to look good at your class reunion, but also to maintain mental acuity as you age. Weight gain with each passing year can elevate your blood sugar, which in turn can increase your risk of memory loss. Too much glucose in the blood means too little glucose in the body's cells, including brain cells responsible for short-term memory. Drop pounds to bring blood sugar back to a healthy level.
- Instead of sending a traditional thank-you card, insert your message of thanks into a small picture frame. If it's going to a close friend or family member, consider including a photo of the birthday child (or adult!). The recipient will really appreciate the extra effort.

Grace Notes
for August . . .

Summer Vacations

Health

Vacations—with their long travel time, limited access to kitchens, and finicky eaters who appreciate a familiar meal—can translate into lots of fast food. With healthier choices on the menu, however, grabbing a bite on the fly need not be a diet disaster. If you choose a salad, be sure to top it with low-fat dressing, as the others may be laden with fat and calories.

Fitness

Don't leave your exercise regimen at home! Make it a point to travel with your own portable "gym." Tote along a jump rope for cardio and a resistance band for strength training. For each day you're away, create an exercise plan. If possible, scout vacation destinations for walking routes. Perhaps the city you're visiting has a great park or network of walking trails. For every week you're away, plan to devote three whole days to active pursuits.

Home

Get your home in order so you can leave it with an easy mind. Arrange for your mail to be held at the post office or picked up by a neighbor. Have your plants watered, your animals cared for, and your house looked in on at regular intervals. Give copies of contact information to a trusted friend.

Family

Keep traveling fun for everyone! Pack a special bag with vacation goodies for each of your children. Goodies should include fun activities, such as coloring books, crayons, markers, and books, as well as edible treats such as Goldfish crackers, granola bars, and juice boxes.

Self

Fraught with logistical and interpersonal challenges, air-tight itineraries, or budget constraints, vacations are often less than relaxing. Make it a point to spend at least one afternoon of your time off alone. Whether a solitary stroll on the beach, a window-shopping excursion, or an afternoon spent reading a good book, give yourself a moment to relax and focus less on "doing" and more on "being."

September

Labor Day

In 1894 the first Monday of September became an
official American holiday. Labor Day was born out
of organized protest marches from disgruntled
employees who were fighting against the poor
working conditions and the low pay endemic at the
time. Today, we honor their commitment and
contribution to the strength, prosperity,
and well being of our country.

Health

- Have a cup of tea this Labor Day morning! Did you know
  that simply by switching your pot of coffee to a pot of tea
  at breakfast, adding an apple to your lunch, and slicing
  some onions into your dinner salad, you may be
  knocking down your risk of heart disease by one-third,
  according to a medical study in the Netherlands? The
  magic ingredient in these foods appears to be
  flavonoids, natural components of all plants, fruits, and
  vegetables, but the three foods in which flavonoids have
  the highest ability to fight LDL ("bad" cholesterol) turn
  out to be tea, apples, and onions! Drinking a few cups of
  tea, and eating an apple and about ⅛ cup of onions daily

should make you 32 percent less likely to die of heart disease than those who do not consume these foods, according to this Dutch research.

- Labor Day means back to school, and back to after-school snacks. Before you turn in tonight, take a few minutes to wash and slice fruits and veggies. Store them in see-through containers at the front of your fridge so your starving students can help themselves.

- On the first day of school, give your family a vitamin-rich send-off with fresh-squeezed orange juice. Studies show that kids who start their day with a healthy breakfast, including fresh fruit juice, have improved memory and creativity. In addition, in a study at the University of Tier in Germany, subjects who had high blood levels of vitamin C stayed calmer during stressful situations.

- Follow autumn's colorful cues and give up all white foods this season. Replace white bread, white rice, white potatoes, and even cream sauces with whole grains, sweet potatoes, and low-fat, dairy-free sauces.

- If you work at an office that typically shares sugary treats or candy dishes, make it a point on the Friday *before* Labor Day weekend to recruit coworkers to band together for better health at the office. One solution might be starting a community fruit bowl and lunchtime walks.

- Need another reason to tuck into a Jonagold, Macintosh, or Fuji? (All three varieties of apple are particularly good for snacking.) The amazing apple banishes bad breath. The crisp fibers of this fruit gently scrub teeth as you chew, while the pectin neutralizes food odors. Your mouth will feel fresh and clean.

SIMPLE SUGGESTIONS FOR CELEBRATORY MEALS

Labor Day means that barbecue season is winding down, so take advantage of the last golden days of summer and make a feast at the grill. Or host a traditional clambake, with clams, lobster, chowder, and shrimp boils. Serve with boiled potatoes, pasta-and-pea salad, and garden-vegetable ratatouille. For dessert, consider peach cobbler, lemon sponge cake, or an all-American apple pie with cheddar cheese. Toast your fellow hardworking Americans with a frosty margarita, frozen daiquiri, Hurricane, or a Cape Cod or mai-tai punch.

Fitness

- Instead of planning your usual end-of-summer family get-together around the backyard picnic table, plan to meet friends at a neighborhood tennis court. You can tote along a well-stocked picnic basket, but by shifting the focus from food to friendly competition, you're far less likely to stuff yourself.
- If you are planning to have guests visit this holiday weekend, ask them to bring their bicycles. Scout a nearby bike path, and schedule an after-lunch bike tour.
- Fall means fall sports. Organize a game of flag football with your kids, or pump up the soccer ball and do some

passing drills. If your kids are part of a school or recreational league, help them sharpen their skills as you burn calories.

· Saddle up for fun this Labor Day weekend. Arrange for a riding lesson at a local stable if you're not too confident on a horse. Although riding may look like it's more work for the horse than the human, it's actually a great form of exercise. It strengthens core muscles, improves balance and posture, and tones your inner thighs and butt. Moreover, it gets you outside in some of the most glorious weather of the year.

FITNESS FOCUS: BACK

With a nod to the backbreaking labor undertaken by our hardworking forebears, use August to strengthen the muscles of your back! Having a strong, flexible back is the best way to ensure that you won't be saddled with debilitating back pain.

· Lying on your stomach with your arms stretched out in front of you and your hips pressed to the ground, use your lower back to lift your chest and arms off the ground. (Hint: You should look like Superman flying through the air.) Hold for one count, then lower. Do three sets of ten.

· Hop on the rowing machine at the gym and do ten minutes. Make certain your movements are smooth, slow, and controlled. Avoid yanking on the crossbar, don't lock your knees or elbows, and go slowly until you get the hang of it.

- Bent-over row: Standing with feet about hip distance apart, with knees slightly bent, lean over at the waist so that your torso is at a 45-degree angle from your hips. Grasp a weighted body bar with a wide overhand grip. Keeping your knees soft, squeeze your shoulder blades together behind your back, bend your elbows, and slowly pull up bar to your waist. Repeat eight times.

HOME Décor

- Revive your garden with a blaze of bright chrysanthemums. Replace pots of fading summer blooms with urns of these hardy flowers. First grown as flowering herbs by the ancient Chinese, mums were believed to contain the power of life.
- For your Labor Day shindig, think casual and rustic. Use a basket of fruit for your centerpiece, chill bottled beverages in empty terra-cotta pots, and co-opt the top of your picnic hamper as an extra table.
- Install a window box outside of your home office or kitchen window and fill it up with brightly colored autumn flowers.
- Welcome fall inside by replacing your summer floral tablecloth with one in rich autumnal hues. Think saffron, burgundy, cranberry, gold, and sienna. Consider changing the covers on your throw pillows to continue the theme. If you have a fireplace, set it "ablaze" with a flat of flame-colored mums.

- An easy and inexpensive way to update your kitchen this fall is to change the drawer pulls and cabinet knobs. Home and hardware stores feature a wide range of styles, everything from basic brass to rustic wrought iron to wildly whimsical designs.

HOMEkeeping and Organization

- Take advantage of the warm weather to scrub outdoor toys and furniture. You'll want your patio looking nice if you're having guests over for Labor Day, and once folks are gone, your things will be ready to put away. If you know you don't have sufficient storage space to stow furniture over the winter, invest in plastic furniture tarps this weekend so you can have them on hand at the first sign of cold weather.

- Establish a school bin for each of your children to hold school library books, papers, and homework due, etc. Place fabric-lined baskets labeled with your children's names on a shelf within their reach. Choose a shelf in a convenient location, ideally somewhere near the entryway. If you use your garage as an entrance to your home, create a space there. You can even hang pegs on the walls to hold kid's book bags.

- Save a clean, empty pizza box (one for each of your school-age kids) and convert it into a catchall for oversize artwork. Each child can decorate his or her own "portfolio" with construction paper, remnants of leftover wallpaper or contact paper, stickers, drawings, and letters. Label the front of each box with their names, then keep them stacked on a closet shelf.

- Rather than hanging each and every one of your child's masterpieces, keep the memories (and not the clutter) by photographing your child's artwork and displaying it in an album.

- When you purchase school supplies, make a point to buy cheap markers. Your kids are going to leave the caps off whether you buy a fancy $12 assortment or a $3 set.

- Make several copies of any medical forms your child needs for school. Chances are she'll need copies for various after-school activities as well, Girl Scouts, soccer, etc. It's also a good idea to keep a set on hand in case of emergency.

- To remove ballpoint ink from new school clothes, place the stain facedown on paper towels. Treat from the back with cleaning fluid or dry-cleaning solvent. Keep changing the paper towel underneath to absorb the ink. Dab on a few drops of isopropyl rubbing alcohol if still needed. Once dry, launder as usual.

- Apples make an excellent natural odor eliminator! To knock out pesky odors in your home or car, simply place a couple of apple halves in these areas for six hours to absorb the smell.

- When you get your Labor Day photos developed, pick up a new scrapbook and organize all your summer photos. You'll be glad you did, before the next rush of picture taking during the fall holiday season.

Family

- Help your kids learn about their own family "labor force" by having them visit Mom or Dad at the office. Talk to them about careers, and encourage them to think about what they might like to be when they grow up. Give them a sense that their choices are boundless.
- Take your children apple picking this month. Upon returning home, put them "in charge" of preparing homemade applesauce or apple pie. Children are eager kitchen helpers when given the opportunity.
- Help kids adjust to new routines by easing into them gradually. The week before Labor Day, start putting the kids to bed a little earlier. Overcome potential objections with an extra-special bedtime ritual: a new

---

READER TO READER

An overworked single mom, I learned from Simple Steps how to bring some balance into my life. I am now proud to say that I can enjoy my days off without the guilt I used to feel about having homework to do for my business. My most important job is raising my children, so when a holiday gives us a day off together, we spend that time together and cherish every minute.

—Anna G., Dover, Delaware

story from the library, a favorite lullaby, a prayer to share, and lots of hugs and kisses. This week start limiting your child's intake of sugar, especially toward the late afternoon, so he or she can sleep better.

- To ease the morning rush on the first day of school, set the breakfast table the night before. Pack lunches, settle on first-day outfits and all accessories, and get kids in bed early!

CHITCHAT

When our children were just beginning preschool, the three of us started a fun Labor Day tradition to help ease our children into new school routines, one we continue year after year. The day before school starts, we plan an hour-and-a-half-long "back to school" dinner party with our three families . . . usually consisting of home-made pizza, a tossed salad, and a special back-to-school cake. The kids even exchange small gifts, like school supplies, coloring books, or new lunch totes. Before everyone parts, we take an annual group photograph. It's become a fun celebration the kids look forward to, one that fosters excitement about the school year ahead!

— Lisa, Linda, and Beverly

Self

- Loath to let go of your late-summer glow? Reach for some light facial bronzers with SPF 15. It's far better for your skin than a true tan, and you can keep your sun-kissed look even when the weather grows nippy.
- Similarly, chase away back-to-work/end-of-summer blues by giving yourself a fun fall activity to which you can look forward. Go "leaf peeping" in the country, plan a wine-tasting trip with your spouse, or convince your sister to host Thanksgiving this year!
- This fall, start dressing for success. You need not dress *up*, but in a way that's neat, put-together, and appropriate to your lifestyle. Retire old sweats and paint-stained T-shirts. We all feel better when we look better. With this in mind, take a look inside your closet. Pack away white shoes and anything else that's out of season, purge the clothes you no longer wear, fix the clothes that need mending, and organize the clothes you still intend to wear.
- You laid out clothes for the kids; now do the same for yourself. Starting tonight, get in the habit of choosing

---

FUN FACTS: LABOR DAY

According to the American College of Occupational and Environmental Medicine, the average American spends over eighteen hundred hours each year at work.

tomorrow's outfit. You'll begin the day feeling that much more in control.

- Since today is Labor Day, take a moment to look at how many hours you spend at work. America is a nation of workaholics. Are you feeling burned-out, overstressed, pulled in a million directions? This Labor Day, figure out ways you can work smarter, not harder. On their deathbeds, few people say, "I wish I'd spent more time at work!"

- Likewise, if you're unhappy in your job, or are thinking about heading back to work, changing jobs, or even launching a new career, set aside a few hours this week to spend some time strategizing. Go online and do some research on continuing education, head to the library for a book on résumé writing, even brush up your networking skills at your end-of-summer barbecue!

- Once you've bundled the kids off to an early bedtime, practice good sleep hygiene yourself. Don't expect to nod off easily if you pay your bills or exercise vigorously just before turning in. Now that autumn has arrived, institute some soothing nighttime rituals. Soak in a lavender-scented bath, sip chamomile or valerian tea, and retire with a good book.

- Write out a positive message on a small notecard and slip it into your breakfast cereal bowl or coffee mug to greet you in the morning. Starting your day with a "You are amazing!" or "You look beautiful today!" will perk up your whole day. And while you're at it, slip a note into your husband's mug or children's breakfast dishes too!

Grace Notes
for September . . .

Grandparents' Day

In 1978, President Jimmy Carter made Grandparents'
Day a national holiday. September was chosen to
signify the "autumn years" of life.

Health

Cook up a favorite family recipe tonight for dinner. Perhaps
your grandmother's incredible lasagna or her famous
chicken soup. If you don't have any old family recipes on
hand, why not make something retro? Even if your grandparents are no longer in your life, they are always in your
heart. Turkey meat loaf and mashed sweet potatoes provide
old-fashioned comfort with a healthy twist!

Fitness

If your parents or grandparents are alive, why not take this
opportunity to encourage them to stay fit? Studies have

shown that the benefits of a strong body are considerable at any age, and there are plenty of gentle kinds of exercise for seniors. Water exercise is a fine cardio workout, gentle on the joints, and delightfully sweat free.

Home

Dust off old family photo albums and take a trip down memory lane. Display old pictures this week. If you can, create a wall of ancestors, with family photos old and new. Sketch a family tree to mat and frame.

Family

Grandparents' Day was made for family gatherings, so round up Grams, Gramps, and nearby relatives for coffee and dessert. Play board games with everyone from the youngest relative to the oldest grandparent and share stories of ancestors past.

Self

If you can't see your grandmother or grandfather today, be sure to give them a call, or sit down and write them a letter. Drop by an elderly neighbor's house with a basket of cookies. Use Grandparents' Day to demonstrate love and respect for *all* our elders, whether or not they happen to be related to you.

Rosh Hashanah

Rosh Hashanah marks the beginning of the
Jewish calendar, a happy time of renewal, discovery,
and a chance to begin again in the New Year.

Health

Go easy on the challah bread (scrumptious as it is), and instead fill up on the traditional carrots, dates, pomegranate
seeds, and, of course, apples! Purchase a dozen apples,
each one a different variety, to symbolize each month of the
new year. Slice them up with a honey dip to bring on a sweet
year.

Fitness

Honor the New Year by trying something completely new,
like belly dancing or capoeira.

Home

In the spirit of "Hiddur Mitzvah," which means to enhance the act or ritual, set a gorgeous table tonight. Use your finest linen, best dishes, and holiday silver.

Family

Sit down with your children or grandchildren and make New Year's cards out of construction paper and colored markers. Drop them into friends' mailboxes or send them to faraway friends and family.

Self

Go shopping! It is traditional to purchase a new outfit, symbolic of your renewal. New Year . . . new you!

October

Halloween

Halloween dates back to the pre-Christian Celtic New Year's festival, All Hallows' Eve. On All Hallows' Eve, it was believed that the spirits of the dead were permitted to return for one night. To scare away these spirits, the Celts would light huge bonfires and wear animal skins (the first Halloween costumes). When the Irish migrated to America, they brought Halloween costumes and made candlelit jack-o'-lanterns out of pumpkins. The celebration quickly evolved into an American tradition of frolic and fun!

Health

- October marks the start of comfort-food season, and eating oatmeal for breakfast has been found to curb hunger and speed weight loss. Scientists compared participants who ate 350 calories of dry cereal to those who ate 350 calories of oatmeal and found that the oatmeal group consumed 30 percent less at lunch and felt less hungry throughout the day.
- This year purchase Halloween candy that you don't like— you'll be far less likely to sample the snacks you give to trick-or-treaters. Or forgo candy altogether, and give out mini granola bars or individually wrapped boxes of raisins.

- Pack your kids a special Halloween lunch on the thirty-first. Use a metal cookie cutter to press a sandwich into the shape of a pumpkin. Enclose a bag of grapes with a sticky note that reads, "eyeballs," and a bag of carrot sticks labeled "bones." Fill their thermoses with a delicious, nutritious "witches' brew," a smoothie made of mangoes, bananas, blueberries, and apple juice.

- Once the pumpkin carving is complete, don't forget to roast the pumpkin seeds! They're a healthy Halloween treat.

- On Halloween night, low-simmer some hot apple cider in an open saucepan on the stove. Throw in cloves, cinnamon, nutmeg, orange slices, and lemon rinds. Not only will your home smell fabulous, you'll have warm refreshments to serve the moms and dads of the trick-or-treaters who come calling!

- Bobbing for apples tonight? Be sure to wash them thoroughly. Apples, like cherries, grapes, pears, raspberries, strawberries, celery, green beans, lettuce, and winter squash, are high-residue foods—meaning they retain pesticides. When available, try to purchase organic produce, which contains fewer pesticides.

- Check your children's candy bag thoroughly with an eye toward health as well as safety. Sneak away any candy that you think is just too bad for their teeth. Throw it out so you are not tempted to eat it yourself!

- Establish a rule that once trick-or-treat candy has been inspected, it gets put away, either inside the pantry or on a high cabinet, to be doled out one piece per day.

Continue until the kids forget about the treats and stop asking for them. Toss the leftovers.

- If you're heading out to a Halloween party, wear a snug-fitting costume. You'll be less likely to overindulge when you can feel your waistband.

RECIPE BOX: PUMPKIN PANCAKES

Combine ½ cup canned pumpkin, ½ cup low-fat vanilla yogurt, ¼ tsp. baking soda, 1 large egg yolk, and ¼ cup whole-wheat flour. Spray cooking spray in a nonstick skillet and heat over medium heat. Spoon in ⅓ cup batter for each pancake and flip when the tops are covered with bubbles and edges are just turning brown. Pour on 100 percent maple syrup and enjoy on Halloween morning!

SIMPLE SUGGESTIONS FOR CELEBRATORY MEALS

In addition to the ubiquitous candy that accompanies the holiday, nothing says Halloween like foods made from pumpkin. Some favorites are pumpkin soup, toasted pumpkin seeds, pumpkin bread, pumpkin ravioli, pumpkin pancakes, and, of course, pumpkin pie. Apples are another autumn staple, so even if you're not bobbing for them, make certain they figure heavily in your Halloween meal. Try purple cabbage with apples, mulled apple cider, baked apples with cinnamon, or apple cobbler. If you anticipate little time to cook as you accompany your goblins on their rounds, consider a slow-cooked hearty chicken soup with crusty bread. Don't forget the hot chocolate!

Fitness

- Make a bet with a friend or your spouse that you can stick to a regular exercise program for the seven weeks between Halloween and Christmas. In a Michigan State University study, people who bet $40 that they could stick with their program for six months had a 97 percent success rate. Less than 20 percent of those who didn't bet stuck to their routines.

- If you are hosting this year's Halloween party, keep yourself away from the food platters by participating in the games with the kids. Bobbing for apples, sack racing, or running the pumpkin piñata station helps preclude nibbling.

- Gather friends and neighborhood kids for a Halloween celebration that doesn't involve candy. Meet at a roller rink or ice arena for a "Monster Mash" skating party.

- What activity is more quintessentially autumnal than raking leaves? The good news is that it's also great exercise.

- Adopt an easy wash-and-wear hairstyle. The new 'do won't make you more fit, but when hair isn't a hassle, you're far more inclined to squeeze in a midday workout.

FITNESS FOCUS: CHEST

Chest exercises won't make you look like a bodybuilder (or like your son's Incredible Hulk Halloween getup) but they *can* give you a lift in a strategic spot.

- Bench press: lying on a fitness bench, grasp 5- or 8-pound dumbbells in each hand. Beginning with arms bent and your hands just slightly outside your shoulders, press your arms straight up. Avoid locking your elbows, and make sure that when your arms are extended, the weights are directly above your chest and not your face. Think about *squeezing* the muscles of your chest. Do three sets of fifteen.
- Chest fly: Lying on a fitness bench with your feet resting on the floor, grasp weights and extend your arms straight above your chest as you did for the bench press. This time, however, keep your palms facing in. Keeping a slight bend in your elbows, open your arms out, as if you are hugging a giant ball. Lower your hands until they are parallel with your shoulders; then, engaging your chest muscles, squeeze them shut again. Do three sets of fifteen.
- Chest push-ups: This variation on the traditional push-up can be done on your knees (a modified push-up) or on your toes. Instead of beginning with your hands directly beneath your shoulders with your fingers pointing straight ahead, place your hands wider than shoulder distance apart on the floor with your fingers pointing outward. In this position, do three sets of ten

push-ups. Don't be discouraged if you can't do so many at first—these are hard! Start with three sets of three if you have to, and do them three times a week. Every two weeks, add one more to each set. You'll be doing ten before you know it.

HOME Décor

- Decorate your front door with the rich symbols of an autumn harvest. Post a cornstalk beside the door or hang a cluster of colored Indian corn. Display a colorful array of pumpkins and gourds in a decorative outdoor urn.
- Use assorted gourds and small pumpkins as candleholders for your mantel this Halloween. Simply carve out a cylinder deep and wide enough to insert the end of a tapered candle.
- A lit jack-o'-lantern smells far sweeter if you sprinkle a little cinnamon and nutmeg on the skin inside around the candle. The heat from the candle creates a delightful aroma.
- Perk up a faded garden with an old-fashioned scarecrow. Have each person in your family provide one piece of clothing to be stuffed with straw.
- Line your walkway with Halloween luminaries. Fill brown paper bags with two inches of sand, and sink a votive candle securely in the bottom.
- Capture the spirit of Halloween. Hang a skeleton in your

**CRAFT BOX:
SMILEY PUMPKIN-FACE GARLAND**

Dress up your mantel or family room wall with a garland made of orange plastic plates. Simply turn them upside down and paint on jack-o'-lantern faces (triangle eyes and nose) with black permanent marker. Glue on little green felt "stems" and tie the plates together with green yarn.

foyer. Hang a little witch in the corner of your kitchen (said to bring good luck).

- Cluster large collections of Halloween decorations together. Small ceramic pumpkins can be gathered in front of real pumpkins for a festive look. An indoor collection of whimsical scarecrows can be clustered together at the base of the foyer stairs or on a fireplace hearth.

- When lighting candles this Halloween night, be sure to use unscented candles or ones that are all the same scent (such as pumpkin spice) so that the aroma is not too unbearable.

- Adorn your home with earth tones and feel more grounded. According to the principles of feng shui, the colors of autumn are also the colors of practicality and reliability—so decorating with brown, russet, and beige can help keep you from feeling overwhelmed.

HOMEkeeping and Organization

- The week or even the day before Halloween, carve your pumpkins into jack-o'-lanterns. Too much earlier and they may rot before the big day.
- Attention ghouls with green thumbs: Halloween marks the last day to plant your spring bulbs for the new year, so get busy!
- Halloween typically coincides with daylight savings time. Use this time to change batteries in your home smoke/fire detectors and discuss the importance of fire safety with your children. (National Fire Safety Week is the first week of October.)

READER TO READER

I used to feel completely overwhelmed with clutter and have no desire to pull out pesky little holiday decorations to add to it all. But the Simple Steps program reminded me that this is a journey, not a destination. I faithfully continue decluttering with that one drawer, cabinet, or closet every week. I know now that I'm in control and it's okay if decorations add to the clutter for the moment of a holiday like Halloween, because in that moment, they're really not clutter but family keepsakes to warm our spirits.

—Mary M., Walnut Creek, California

- If you're hosting the neighborhood Halloween party, make sure that the invitations have a specific start and end time on them to prevent an overflow of guests, goodies, and adrenaline. Short and sweet is best.
- The day after Halloween is the best time to scour discount stores for organizational bins for storing away this year's décor. You'll not only get most of them on sale, but you can get them color-coordinated for the holiday (green and orange bins are still available before the red and green colors of Christmas move onto store shelves).

Family

- Designate the first Sunday of October family costume-planning day. Costumes should be ordered or made promptly, with a strict rule for *no* mind changing after planning day. This gives you the rest of the month to pick up any necessary costume accessories. Skip costumes with big shoes kids could trip on. Opt for painted faces, hats, and wigs over masks that obscure kids' vision. And always make sure your costumes are flame-resistant.
- Pin a label with your child's name, address, and phone number to the inside of his costume or candy bag in case he strays away while trick-or-treating in a big group.
- Affix reflective or glow-in-the-dark tape to the back of your child's costume, and be sure to bring a flashlight when trick-or-treating in the dark.

- Play a few Victorian Halloween games at your Halloween bash! If bobbing for apples seems too messy or wet, hang apples from ribbons attached to the ceiling and see who can get his or her teeth into his or her apple first. Once that's done, have each guest try to peel his or her apple in one long unbroken peel . . . the person with the longest strip wins. Then have everyone toss the strip over their right shoulder. According to Victorian tradition, the letter the peel forms (use your imagination here) is the first initial of the person he or she is going to marry.

CHITCHAT

For families with small children, it's important to try to shift emphasis from the candy to the Halloween festivities to follow. In my home that means a hot bath after the chilly neighborhood walk and a fun peek at some of the Polaroid or digital photos taken earlier as we put them into our little Halloween family album. Then it's fresh-popped popcorn and a Halloween movie (*It's the Great Pumpkin, Charlie Brown,* anyone?). It provides a nice wind-down to an exciting holiday.

—Lisa Lelas

- Take your family to a pumpkin patch and see who can find the roundest, the smallest, or the brightest orange pumpkin. The winner gets crowned with a gold-foil paper crown as King or Queen Jack for the day! If you can't get to a pumpkin patch, many city markets and produce stands also load up on pumpkins during the month of October. Don't forget your cameras!

- Want more treats than tricks this Halloween? Why not bring your family to a day at an amusement park? Many parks celebrate the holiday in spooky style. At Six Flags parks, you can celebrate Fright Fest with a variety of hair-raising activities, including screaming contests and Halloween weddings!

- Rent *The Wizard of Oz* this Halloween weekend for a family movie night.

- Allow yourself fifteen minutes of alone time with your spouse to sit and enjoy a cup of herb tea or a glass of wine after work to unwind, catch up on each other's days and get yourself ready for the doorbell parade that's about to begin!

Self

- Plan a day of precious "me" time before or after Halloween. Whether you just sit quietly with a cup of tea and read a novel, visit a ceramic studio and make pottery, or take off a day from work and go for an autumn hike, reserve a day in this busy season to focus on you.

- Not all Halloween masks need to be scary—smooth on this soothing egg-white mask and reduce laugh lines.

According to Seth Matarasso, MD, associate clinical professor of dermatology at the University of California School of Medicine, egg whites on your face temporarily tighten and flatten the appearance of wrinkles. Simply beat an egg white until it's frothy and apply it over your skin. Let it dry for five minutes, then rinse first with warm water, then cool water. Use a fresh egg white for each application and don't apply too close to your eyes.

- If Halloween makeup has made your skin break out, zap your blemishes the natural way. Make a paste of 1 tsp. each lemon juice, apple cider vinegar, and salt. Apply to the pimple and let it sit for fifteen minutes and then rinse. The lemon juice gently bleaches the blemish as the vinegar solution eases inflammation.

- Pop a spine-tingling suspense novel or supernatural thriller into your Walkman this month, and listen to a book on tape during your morning walk.

- When trolling the vintage clothing stores for kids' costumes, don't forget to keep an eye out for yourself. A charming beaded purse, fitted forties-style jacket, rhinestone brooch, or glorious pair of gloves could prove a perfect complement to your everyday wardrobe.

- Wear your opal earrings today! October's birthstone— long known as the wish stone for its alleged ability to foster romance and grant wishes—is supposed to be lucky for all birth signs when worn this month.

- If wool-sweater weather gives you dry, itchy skin, drink oolong tea. Japanese researchers found that people who

drink three cups of oolong tea daily relieved the
symptoms of atopic dermatitis.

- Even if you are not planning to wear a Halloween
costume tonight, put on a fun accessory, such as Mickey
Mouse ears or a witch's hat, and jump into the spirit of
the day with your children!

Grace Notes
for October . . .

Columbus Day

The first recorded celebration of Columbus Day
in the United States took place on October 12, 1792,
commemorating the three hundredth anniversary
of Columbus's landing in the Americas.

Health

In honor of Christopher Columbus's seafaring voyages, visit
your local fish market and pick up some gifts from the sea.
October also brings the National Shrimp Festival, a big celebration in the U.S. gulf states—so be sure to incorporate
some into tonight's meal.

Fitness

Take your family on your very own voyage of discovery. Walk
a nature trail and encourage kids to collect different kinds of
pinecones, acorns, and leaves. Identify their species by

looking them up in a field guide to local flora once you get home.

Home

Check out Columbus Day seasonal sales at local stores to get a great bargain on a backyard hammock. Hammocks were introduced to Europeans from the New World.

Family

Go online or to the library, and share stories with your children about Christopher Columbus. Help your child create her own ship model (*Niña*, *Pinta*, and *Santa Maria*) using easy-to-find materials like clay, milk cartons, or Popsicle sticks.

Self

Indulge in a chocolate dessert today. Chocolate was also introduced to Europeans from Mesoamerica, where it was the food of royalty!

Yom Kippur

Ten days after Rosh Hashanah comes Yom Kippur, the
Jewish Day of Atonement. One of the holiest and
most solemn days of the Jewish calendar, it is given
over to fasting and prayers for forgiveness.

Health

Drink lots of water during your daylong fast. Avoid getting a
caffeine-withdrawal headache on Yom Kippur by cutting
down on coffee and tea in the weeks leading up to it. Don't
stuff yourself before your fast; it won't make the day go any
more quickly. When you break your fast, don't gorge yourself. Your body's metabolism will have slowed in response to
the lack of food, and will be less able to process a huge meal.

Fitness

If exercise today feels inappropriate, focus instead on
breathing. Take three ten-minute-long "breathing breaks."

Inhale for a count of four, retain breath for a count of two, and exhale for a count of four. You'll feel calm, refreshed, and centered.

Home

In the spirit of fasting, keep decorations to a minimum.

Family

On this day of atonement, encourage your children to ask for and grant forgiveness freely. Learning to say you're sorry and accept apologies are important lessons for people of all ages.

Self

As part of a traditional cleansing ritual, write down any wrongdoings over the past year on bits of paper and toss them into a nearby river. Reconcile with God, with yourself, and with others. And smile: it's going to be a great year!

November

Thanksgiving

Originally designated by President Abraham Lincoln,
Thanksgiving Day was not actually declared a national
holiday until 1941 by President Franklin D. Roosevelt.
Just as the Pilgrims gave thanks for their family,
friends, and their first bountiful feast, in the spirit
of our ancestors, we too give thanks as part
of this American tradition.

Health

- Drink lots of water during the days leading up to and
  after a big meal to help keep your energy up, your
  appetite satisfied, and extra calories moving out.
- If you are making the holiday feast, plan your menu and
  make a master shopping list. Don't buy anything that is
  not on it.
- Cranberries aren't just for relish: Wake up and treat
  yourself to a glass of organic cranberry juice on
  Thanksgiving morning.
- Homemade isn't always healthier. Some ready-made
  cooking sauces can save you time . . . and calories! Look
  for sauces with less than 3 grams of fat per serving.

- If you're a "from scratch" cook and store-bought just won't do, keep the creaminess but lose the fat in your sauces by using 2 percent evaporated milk in place of cream in recipes. Evaporated milk has been treated by a heating process, reducing its moisture content so it has a thicker and creamier consistency. It's approximately 50 percent more concentrated in energy and nutrients. It is an excellent source of protein and calcium and is fortified with vitamins A and D.
- Similarly, to reduce fat in baking try buttermilk in place of sour cream, butter, or margarine. Buttermilk is made by adding "friendly" bacterial cultures to (usually) low-fat milk. The bacterial culture produces its unique flavor, aroma, acidity, and thick texture. Despite its name, butter is not added!

FUN FACTS: THANKSGIVING

Two hundred seventy-two million turkeys are raised in the United States every year, and 1.25 billion pounds of sweet potatoes are harvested each year, a large percentage of these sold during the month of November.

- Don't diet on Thanksgiving Day. Your goal should be to maintain weight, not to lose it. Plan to eat just a little bit of everything . . . don't make anything completely off-limits. Choose fiber before sweets to fill you up,

and choose protein over sugary treats to keep you full
longer.

· Make Thanksgiving Day one of the few planned-upon
"fiesta" days of the year and you can anticipate the joy of
eating your favorite treats, says Dr. Neal Bernard at the
Santa Barbara Institute for Medical Nutrition and
Healthy Weight. Simply promise yourself that no matter
what you're eating, you'll measure out only a single
portion.

· Don't blow your healthy eating habits en route to your
Thanksgiving Day destination. Avoid mindless
munching through the miles during a long car trip by
filling individual-size plastic bags with 100 calories'
worth of favorite treats. Allow yourself (and everyone
else in the car) one snack bag midmorning and one
midafternoon!

· Bring along healthy alternatives if you are not hosting
the holiday meal. By offering to bring a favorite low-
calorie dish, you will know that there will be at least one
"safe" item available.

· Wear a belt to dinner. You will have a constant reminder
of your determination not to overindulge this
Thanksgiving.

· Let Thanksgiving time be the reminder you need to quit
smoking if you are still sneaking those puffs every day.
It's the single most important thing you can do for your
health. The Great American Smokeout is usually the
third week of November (close to the Thanksgiving Day
holiday). Visit www.cancer.org for ideas on how to kick

the habit once and for all. Then you will surely have something to be grateful for this Thanksgiving.

SIMPLE SUGGESTIONS FOR CELEBRATORY MEALS

Some of the traditional foods that we've inherited from the folks at the first Thanksgiving include squash, corn, and wheat. Neither turkey nor cranberries adorned the Pilgrims' or Indians' plates, but they've since come to be standard Thanksgiving fare. Goose, duck, ham, and seafood have all been featured as main courses on the third Thursday in November, along with yams, squash, maize, beans, wild and brown rice, carrots, and green beans. Consider cranberry butter, cranberry orange relish, cranberry chutney, or ginger-cranberry sauce. An accompanying salad can nicely round out the meal: Think asparagus-and-mushroom salad, warm spinach salad, or a green bean–and-bacon salad. For dessert: sweet-potato pie, cream pies, or pecan pies are always favorites. The simplest Thanksgiving menu can be marvelous, so long as the folks who sit down before it are grateful to share a meal with friends and loved ones.

Fitness

- At this busy time of year, sneak in as much extra activity as possible. When doing your Thanksgiving grocery shopping, return your shopping cart to the store entrance instead of abandoning it in the parking lot.

Walk to the mailbox to mail a letter rather than tossing it into your outbox at work, and try to add just a few more minutes to your morning workout. If you do just one of these little bursts of activity five days a week, you'll drop two to four pounds a year (based on an approximately 140-pound frame). It may not sound like much, but the average woman *gains* one to two pounds a year as she gets older.

- No matter who is hosting Thanksgiving dinner, make sure you've got your sneakers handy. After the turkey, but before the pies, grab some friends or family members for some "walk and talk" activity. You might feel less motivated for heavy desserts!
- Start an exercise-driven Thanksgiving Day tradition. This year, enter your family to walk or run together in a community "Turkey Trot" race on the morning of Thanksgiving Day.
- If you are away from home, scout out a running or walking route first thing in the morning—so you'll know where to go as soon as you find a free hour in the day.
- If you opt to take a break from your normal diet and exercise routines on Thanksgiving, then promise yourself you will get right back on track the day after. Mark it on the calendar and log it into your to-do list to set your plan in stone.
- Rather than simply watching football, get out and play! Host a family football game in the backyard, and aim to have yourself voted MVP.

FITNESS FOCUS: ENDURANCE

In the spirit of our Pilgrim forebears, for whom endurance was a way of life, this month's focus is on increasing our ability to "hang in there." Using the time surrounding Thanksgiving to work on endurance is an easy way to ensure that exercise will not fall by the wayside. Try the following:

- Ramp up your morning walks to include ever-increasing interludes of jogging, or simply increase the distance that you walk in a given time. Keep careful records, and see if you can improve your time.
- At the gym, on the elliptical trainer, bicycle, treadmill, or cardio machine of your choice, alternate periods of high resistance with periods of lower intensity. For example, if on the treadmill you typically walk at a 4.5-mile-an-hour pace for twenty-five minutes, try walking at a 4.5-mile-an-hour pace for five minutes, then a 5-mile-an-hour pace for five minutes, followed by a 4.5-mile-an-hour pace, followed by a 5, and then a 4.5. Think about building your stamina gradually. Simple steps, remember? And this kind of interval training has been proven to be most effective by elite athletes.
- See how long you can sit on an invisible chair! Begin by leaning your back against a wall. Bend your knees and slide your body down as if you're sitting on a chair. Adjust your feet so that they are about hip distance apart, and be sure that your knees are bent at a 90-degree angle, so that your thighs are parallel to the floor and your

lower back is pressed into the wall. Stretch your hands out in front of you, so that they're parallel to your legs. See if you can hold this "chair position" for two minutes, then three, then four. For an extra challenge, hold dumbbells in your hands.

HOME Décor

- Now, after all those orange decorations and jack-o'-lanterns are cleared away, remember that less is more with home décor. Taking a cue from the Pilgrims whom we honor, think simplicity . . . graceful candles lit on the mantel, good china on your table, and the even more precious clay turkey that your five-year-old made.
- Hang a fruit-studded wreath on your front door the week of Thanksgiving to welcome friends and family.
- Steady wobbly candles with double-sided cellophane tape wrapped around the bottom. The tape will stick to the candle and its holder, and will remain invisible in glass candleholders.
- Before relatives arrive, create a corkboard or wall gallery of family photos. It's an easy, fun way to provide a visual diary of the previous year.
- Add a cushioned, nonskid floor mat near the sink and stove to make standing for a long time in one place more comfortable.
- Purchase fresh-cut flowers for your Thanksgiving Day table and place them in a glass vase filled with cranberries and water for a festive look.

HOMEkeeping and Organizing

- If you are hosting dinner at your home, get your kitchen ready at least one week prior to Thanksgiving Day. Organize your pantry, and empty all unnecessary items from the refrigerator to create maximum space for incoming holiday dishes. Clear kitchen counters of nonessential appliances to create ample workspace, and clean your oven a few days before the big event. To get rid of the chemical odors of oven cleaners, bake a few orange peels at 350 degrees for about twenty minutes.
- Stock your pantry without blowing your budget. While you are at the grocery store, scour the high and low shelves for the best bargains on everything from pasta in bulk to soups. The most expensive brands are intentionally stocked at eye level!
- Focus your housecleaning only on those rooms that will be used most often during the holiday: kitchen, dining room, family room, entryway, and guest bath. If friends or family members will be staying with you, don't forget the guest bedroom.
- Freshen up your upholstery before the guests arrive. Pour 2 tsp. of liquid fabric softener and 2 pints of water into a spray bottle, shake, and lightly mist upholstered furniture for a sweet-smelling room. Be sure to do this at least an hour before guests are expected so the furniture has time to dry.
- Spot-treat any gravy stains on your Thanksgiving dinner tablecloth. Blot the spill with paper towels.

Sprinkle on talcum powder, salt, or cornstarch to cover the stain. Let set to absorb grease. Then brush off. Treat with liquid laundry detergent. Wash in the hottest water safe for the fabric.

- Keep even a leftovers-laden refrigerator smelling fresh by scooping ¼ cup of baking soda each into coffee filters, securing them with twist ties, and placing one on each refrigerator shelf. The porous filters absorb odor faster than the baking soda box does. Replace the filter bags once every month.

- Pack up any Thanksgiving holiday décor the day after. Wash and fold any special table linens and napkins to be stored away till next year. Remember, you need to clear the decks for Christmas.

FUN FACTS: THANKSGIVING

Cranberries are sometimes called "bounce berries" by growers in the Northeast. Legend has it that a nineteenth-century New Jersey cranberry farmer had lost one of his legs, so rather than lugging all of his berries down from the hayloft where he kept them, he would pour them down the stairs. The mushy, overripe berries stuck to the stairs, but the perfectly ripe, hard berries bounced down the stairs to the floor below. To this day, major companies, such as Ocean Spray, separate their cranberries by bouncing them over a four-inch barrier!

- The weekend of Thanksgiving is the ideal time to write and seal your holiday greeting cards. Plan on mailing them the first week of December. Before the holiday rush gets you sidetracked, buy any upcoming birthday or anniversary cards and have them ready to mail out. If you are planning a New Year's Eve party, now is the time to send out the invitations.

Family

- If you have younger children sharing your Thanksgiving Day dinner, let them relive the history of the holiday by making simple Pilgrim hats and Indian headdresses out of construction paper and tagboard.
- Have each person at the dinner table—young and old—share reasons they are thankful for living in America.
- When everyone is seated and just before the meal is served, pass around a gratitude journal and ask everyone present to contribute something for which they are thankful. Your guests will leave your home feeling grateful as well as stuffed!
- The week before Thanksgiving, donate a frozen turkey or canned goods to your local soup kitchen.
- If you have teenage kids (age sixteen or older) consider signing up for a Habitat for Humanity program in your state, whereby all volunteers spend a week or a month actually constructing a home to be turned over to an underprivileged family.

- Take your family to your local high school's Thanksgiving Day football game. Beginning the holiday with an activity you all can do together only heightens the meaning of the day.
- After dinner, grab the newspapers and pull out all the holiday shopping sales flyers for the day after Thanksgiving. If you're brave, join the millions of other shoppers around the country at the break of dawn that day for incredible savings. Take your spouse, a parent, a sister, or even a teenage child for another fun postholiday tradition!

CHITCHAT

Several years ago, we started a new family tradition for our Thanksgiving Day dinner. By cutting out cotton fabric and "hemming" it with no-sew/iron-on adhesive strips, we made a table runner that provided the perfect backdrop for family signatures. Each year we use a different-color fabric marker and ask every person present to write down what they are thankful for and sign his or her name. Bearing signatures of everyone from our one-hundred-year-old grandmother to our children (who traced their handprints when they were too young to write), it has become a priceless family heirloom. What a joy it is to look at this visual reminder of so many years' worth of love and gratitude!

—Lisa Lelas and Linda McClintock

READER TO READER

Our family delivers meals for the needy through our local Meals-on-Wheels program on Thanksgiving morning before our festivities begin. It sets the tone for the day and reminds us what we are grateful for.
—Jenn M., Guilford, Connecticut

Self

- Try to go to bed as early as you can the night before Thanksgiving. Adequate sleep will help calm any frazzled nerves over a casserole that didn't come out quite right.
- If you've been up with the turkey since five A.M., indulge in a nap later in the day. If your uncle Hank manages to steal a snooze each year on the sofa while trying to watch football, join him. You deserve it.
- Don't aim to be a superhostess. Ask for help in the kitchen. Share the workload with the rest of your family, or even your guests.
- Feel thankful and improve your overall well-being! According to a study by Robert A. Emmons, Ph.D., professor of psychology at U-Cal at Davis, people who were asked to keep either a daily or weekly report of five things they were grateful for felt more energetic, optimistic, and connected to others than those subjects who were told to record everyday hassles.

READER TO READER

After reading *Simple Steps* and completing the ten-week lifestyle makeover program, I immediately started a gratitude journal and I still cannot believe how it has really changed my life. Taking a few minutes each day to reflect upon all that I am truly grateful for makes every day Thanksgiving Day in my home.

—Laura J., Austin, Texas

- Place a bouquet of fresh roses on your kitchen table on Thanksgiving morning. Aroma therapists use the rich scent of these blooms to relieve anxiety and depression. Add a bit of the emotion-balancing properties of rose essential oil and those crazy holiday mood swings will be a thing of the past!
- If you are traveling this Thanksgiving weekend, stay alert and stay happy! To beat drive-time drowsiness, mix together ½ cup coarse sea salt and several drops of peppermint oil, and then spoon a little into your car's ashtray. Salt keeps the energizing scent of mint going strong for a full week, raising driving alertness and producing a peppy mood that lingers long after you've reached your destination. The scent of peppermint also acts as an appetite suppressant!
- Schedule a warm bath on Thanksgiving evening. You deserve it.

Grace Notes
for November . . .

Veterans Day

A day to honor all veterans of war, past and present.

Health

November is the ideal time of year to get your flu shot—make Veterans Day your reminder to call your doctor and set up an appointment. Coming on the heels of World War I, the influenza epidemic killed between 19 and 35 million people. Happily, nowadays the flu is seldom deadly, but it's still a good idea for people—especially seniors—to get the yearly vaccination.

Fitness

Keep in fighting trim with a military-inspired workout. Sign up for a "boot camp" class at the gym, or rent a videotape.

Home

Hang an American flag from your front porch today.

Family

Share stories of family members or friends who serve or served in the military. Have your kids write letters to American soldiers stationed abroad.

Self

Read a book that brings military history to life. From *The Guns of August* to *All Quiet on the Western Front*, to *The Things They Carried*, get a sense of what it is to be a soldier.

December

Christmas

"Christ" Mass, the Christian celebration of the birth of Jesus, is the most celebrated holiday in America. In addition to the infant Jesus, its most beloved symbol is a plump fellow who sports a snowy white beard and sack full of presents. The original Saint Nicholas is believed to have been the bishop of Myra in fourth-century Turkey. Known for his acts of generosity and kindness, especially toward children, his feast day on December 6 was closely associated with Christmas and was celebrated throughout Europe. Dutch settlers who came to America brought the tradition of venerating Saint Nicholas along with them. And thus the Dutch "Sinterklaas" became the predecessor of the gift-bearing "jolly old elf" we call Santa Claus.

Health

- Put a splash of cranberry juice into your water bottles the week of Christmas for a festive change.
- As an easier alternative to a cocktail party or holiday dinner, consider hosting a holiday tea. On a Sunday afternoon, serve an assortment of teas and coffees, cappuccinos and lattes, and some light snacks.
- Replace a quarter of the oils called for in all your dessert recipes with applesauce to help stay on track this month.

- Whether your Christmas dinner features ham, turkey, beef, or fish, enjoy the entrée but ease up on the gravies and sauces to keep your calorie count down.
- Don't prepare too much food for parties or dinners. This will leave you with too many leftovers, which you will feel obliged to finish. Prepare take-home plates for all your guests or donate leftovers to a food bank.
- Whether you're hosting a party or bringing along a dish to share, try bean dip in place of cheese spread. You'll get more fiber and less fat, fewer calories, and less sodium in every spoonful. A two-tablespoon serving of black bean dip contains just 30 calories.
- Consider making flavored meringue cookies instead of your usual rich and fattening ones. These egg-white confections require less sugar than the average gingerbread man or chocolate-chip cookie, plus they're fat free, so enjoy!
- Fruits like apples and pears poached in wine and liqueur make a sophisticated dessert without using butter or cream. Garnish with fresh blackberries for an elegant presentation.
- Have a piece of fruit before you leave for a holiday party. You'll be better able to resist the temptation to overeat with a full stomach.
- Be a part-time teetotaler at the holiday parties you attend: Alternate alcoholic drinks with sparkling water. Bear in mind that every 4-ounce glass of wine or 6-ounce beer contains approximately 100 calories, mixed drinks have about twice that, and a 4-ounce glass of

spiked eggnog packs a whopping 400 calories. Drinking alcohol also reduces your willpower to resist salty or fatty snacks.

- Commit to meeting at least three new people at each Christmas party you attend. Avoid sitting in a quiet spot by the food table, grazing all night.

- At dinner parties, use a small to medium plate when you serve yourself. Smaller plates will help you stick to smaller portions. Fill your plate with salad and vegetables. After you have finished that plate, if you are still hungry, go back for more fat-filled foods. Be sure to cut all visible fat off meat and remove any skin before consuming.

- Though your holiday revelry may stretch far into the night, don't eat late. Allow yourself at least two hours before bed without eating. Eating too close to bedtime will slow your metabolism, promote weight gain, and interrupt a sound sleep.

- Eat before you go Christmas shopping. Nothing brings on hunger pangs more than a day spent fighting holiday hordes. Bring a few healthy snacks along if you are planning on shopping all day. A snack will curb your appetite, and the appeal of the food courts will be much easier to resist.

- Quell cravings with a cup of tea! Drink a cup of tea whenever you feel the urge to snack on those holiday cookies. Caffeine stimulates the release of a hormone that suppresses appetite and promotes a feeling of fullness.

- Afraid of holiday weight gain? Slip a bottle of peppermint essential oil into your purse. In studies, researchers discovered that women lost an average of five pounds a month just by taking three sniffs of peppermint, banana, or green apple whenever hunger pangs hit. These essential oils appear to stimulate the satiety center of the brain, according to neurologists.

- Feel a winter cold coming on during this busy holiday season? Go ahead and treat yourself to a handful of pecans. Pecans are loaded with zinc, which helps the body produce a protein that stimulates the immune system's virus-fighting cells.

- Laugh away the start of any winter cold. Soothe a sore throat by sticking out your tongue and making funny faces into the mirror. This action stimulates blood to the throat and neck, says Jacob Teitelbaum, MD, helping to decrease inflammation and pain.

- Turn on a humidifier. Cold and flu bugs thrive in dry air. Adding moisture to your home environment weakens the viruses as well as hydrating your nasal passages, so your body is better prepared to fight off germs.

SIMPLE SUGGESTIONS FOR CELEBRATORY MEALS

Arguably the merriest of all the Christian holidays, Christmas has long been celebrated with food, wine, and song. Start your celebratory meal with a golden butternut-squash soup or a tossed salad with toasted chestnuts. For a traditional meal, follow with roasted game hen, roasted goose,

leg of lamb, filet mignon, or baked fish. Possible sides include Brussels sprouts, baked carrots, mashed or roasted
potatoes, or a variety of vegetable salads. Don't forget a teeny
serving of eggnog for a digestif! For dessert, you can't go
wrong with gingerbread cookies, which, dating back to the
Middle Ages, were the first cookies to be associated with
Christmas. Or serve plum pudding, sugared plums, poached
pears, pear brown Betty, mincemeat pies, or candy canes
(which are made in the shape of a J for Jesus), and, of course,
fruitcake.

Fitness

- Consider hiring a personal trainer just to see you
  through the holidays. This is a tricky time of year to keep
  fitness goals on track, and the extra motivation that an
  expert can provide will keep you from skipping workouts
  or overeating.
- Take your kids sledding over winter break: Trudging
  uphill tugging a sled (particularly a sled laden with
  children) is a fine and often overlooked form of
  exercise.
- Consider giving the gift of family recreation for
  Christmas this year. Snowshoes, ice skates, skis, or sleds
  under the tree encourage winter sports fun for the
  remainder of the season.
- If possible, buy your tree from a Christmas tree farm. Be
  sure to cover plenty of ground before you settle on the

perfect tree, climb any available hills for optimal views, then volunteer to be the band saw—wielding woodcutter who cuts it down. Get still more exercise dragging the tree to your car.

- Got a fireplace, or know someone who does? Split some logs for an old-fashioned workout with a lovely reward.
- Put a pair of new sneakers on your Christmas wish list. There's nothing like a bouncy, bright pair of athletic shoes to motivate you to break them in.

FITNESS FOCUS: STABILITY AND BALANCE

Not only is balance a good goal in all areas of our lives, it's particularly precious at this time of year. Strengthen core muscles (abs, obliques, and lower back) with the following:

- Try to remain balanced while sitting on a fitness ball. The incremental adjustments you make emanate from your core muscles.
- Begin on your hands and knees, with your back flat and your neck long and relaxed. Engaging your abdominal muscles to keep you steady, reach your right arm out in front of you as you stretch your left leg out behind you. Hold and balance for a count of eight, then switch sides. Repeat three times.
- The next time you do a set of bicep curls, shoulder presses, or side lifts, do them while standing on one foot. You'll see that you get a more intense workout when not only your arms but also your entire body is working.

HOME Décor

- Take holiday decorations out early this year to enjoy the season to its full capacity. Put up your Christmas tree early to enjoy longer—just be sure to water it daily.
- If the prospect of decking *all* the halls seems overwhelming, consider concentrating on only the rooms in which your family and friends will spend the most time. You don't have to spend a fortune. Sprigs of fresh-cut evergreens dress up a mantel or tabletop in an instant. Display holiday cards on a door frame. Light candles. Scatter bowls of fresh fruit and nuts. Think simple and be creative!
- Decorate a room with candles in the same color for a more elegant, less cluttered look.
- Place tea lights or votives by each setting on your Christmas dinner table.
- Line a bowl with velvet and fill with mixed nuts. This makes a pretty coffee table accent.
- Keep your collection of holiday memories from over the years together in one holiday photo album and display on your coffee table for the entire month of December.
- Purchase a box of inexpensive plain white Christmas tree balls. Cut out several holiday pictures from Christmas cards or wrapping paper and glue them onto the ornaments with decoupage glue using a foam brush. You can also use paint pens to personalize them. These make great gifts!

- Light fragrant candles like gingerbread or balsam pine throughout your home to reinforce the spirit of the Christmas season!
- At work, hang a small wreath on your office door. Get into the spirit!
- Display a Yule log on your hearth, decorated with sprigs of pine, rosemary, and cinnamon sticks. Plan to burn it on Christmas Eve.
- To spread the excitement of the coming of Christmas throughout your home, place a small artificial Christmas tree in each of your children's rooms or in the hallway near their bedrooms. This is theirs to decorate.

HOMEkeeping and Organization

- If you are preparing for a holiday dinner at your home, make a master list of all the things you need, including decorations, food, spirits, and invitations.
- Buy nonperishable food items as early as possible this month to avoid the Christmas rush. Order specialty items (roast, pies, etc.) early to avoid forgetting. As always, prepare as many dishes as you can ahead of time and freeze them.
- If you plan on eating out on the holiday, be sure to make your reservation by the first week in December.
- Likewise, address and mail all Christmas packages and holiday cards before December 7.
- Besides rolls of wrapping paper, keep an ample supply

READER TO READER

Since my children have grown and moved away, I found a simple organizing system for when they come to visit over the holidays. I keep a large, pretty floor basket by the front door for all their miscellaneous items, such as keys, purses, sunglass cases, etc. Now I always know that nothing is left behind at the end of their visit.

—Prue A., Madison, Connecticut

---

of gift bags, boxes, and tissue paper for instant "wraps" needed when unexpected guests drop by. Keep them in a small bin in your gift-wrap center or closet.

· Consider sending electronic greeting cards this year. According to organizer Miriam Mennin, from Miriam Mennin Professional Organizing Services in Cos Cob, Connecticut, Web sites such as BlueMountain.com will not only enable you to send out your Christmas cards in a flash, but they will send you e-mail reminders for birthdays, anniversaries, and even next year's holiday card list for very reasonable annual rates.

· Follow a few Christmas tree tips from professional organizer Faith Maniere of BusyBees Organizing Service of Glastonbury, Connecticut: Save time and consider having your Christmas tree delivered this year. Avoid decorations that make a mess, such as greens that drop needles. Artificial swags are available, reusable, and lovely. Purchase a bigger, more solid tree stand to avoid the possibility of your tree falling down, and discard all old, unloved, or broken ornaments instead of decorating your tree with them.

- Shop on Monday and Tuesday mornings, typically the least busy in retail, and be sure you go armed with a list. You'll save time, energy, and fuel.

FUN FACTS: CHRISTMAS SHOPPING

In 1981, the average household received fifty-nine mail-order catalogs, and by 1991 the number increased 140 percent to 142. If each household canceled just ten mail-order catalogs, it would reduce trash by 3.5 pounds per year. If everybody did this, the stack of canceled catalogs would be two thousand miles high!

- Arrange to spend one weekend before Christmas thinning out the toys. Ask your child to help you decide which toys are no longer age-appropriate and donate them to charity.
- Donate mittens, hats, or even slightly worn coats to the local community shelter this year. Bring your children. It's important for them to see that not everyone has what they do.
- If you're hosting a holiday party, save money by turning down heat as guests begin to arrive. You'll save energy while the extra body heat of your guests warms the room.

- When selecting Christmas tree lights, think small. Small lights have lower wattage, so they are both safer and more energy efficient than larger bulbs.
- Never run extension cords under carpeting or rugs. The cords may overheat and cause a fire.
- Give a unique gift your hostess will cherish forever! Bring a Polaroid instant camera and a small photo album to your next holiday party. Taking pictures of the festivities and immediately placing them into the album makes a great thank-you gift to leave behind.

CHITCHAT

I love to make holiday gift baskets, which I suspect are as fun for me to make as for the recipient to receive. Often my baskets have a theme, such as wine and cheese, gourmet coffee and teas, pedicure and manicure baskets, cooking/baking, or it can be a free-for-all with some home-baked treats such as baked seasoned nuts along with a candle or a book. After I fill the baskets, I cover them in shrink-wrap and attach a homemade bow to the top.

—Linda McClintock

- As you pack away your holiday china after the big day, place a coffee filter or paper towel between each plate so they don't get scratched, cracked, or smashed.

Family

- For each of your children, purchase (or make) a new tree ornament that represents an important event from the past year, such as a ballerina to mark a recital or a sparkly soccer ball to commemorate a successful season. Don't forget to label it with the child's name and the date.
- Turn one evening each week of December into family holiday-craft time. String cranberries for the tree, make construction-paper chains, create homemade Christmas cards, or construct a family gingerbread house. Easy-to-assemble gingerbread kits are available now at most grocery stores. Or for families with young children, try building one with graham crackers and store-bought icing around a small milk carton. Top with assorted candies.
- Institute an "Advent of storybooks." Wrap twenty-five of your favorite holiday stories in holiday paper (they need not be new) and place them in a big basket in your family room. Starting on December 1, have your children select one book as their bedtime story. Conclude on Christmas Eve with Clement C. Moore's classic, *The Night Before Christmas.*
- Save money this Christmas! Have a Kris Kringle present exchange. Have all family members draw a name out of a hat and buy a present for that person only. You may want to set a price limit on gifts.
- Take your children Christmas caroling.
- Instead of a cookie swap, host a toy swap with family

and friends. It's a great way to recycle old or unwanted toys and a cheap way to find some new gifts for your little ones.

- Managing family dynamics at the holidays can be tricky, but you can defuse intergenerational infighting by keeping dinner conversation light and fun. Avoid touchy subjects that will cause tension between family members. If known triggers come up, quickly move the conversation on to something else.
- For a quick holiday treat that kids can make with ease, make ice-cream snowballs. With an ice-cream scoop or a large melon baller, scoop out light ice cream or frozen yogurt to create balls. Roll each ball in coconut and place on a cookie sheet or baking pan lined with waxed paper. Place in freezer until needed. These can be made the day before the dinner.
- One day during the holiday break, schedule a special entertainment outing, such as a holiday concert or a production of *The Nutcracker*.
- During the busy holiday hustle and bustle, designate a "drop everything and read" time in your home, when everyone reads quietly for twenty minutes, including you.
- Go to Church on Christmas Eve. Don't forget whose birthday we are celebrating.

Self

- Place an X on one day each week on your calendar throughout the holiday season. On these days do not schedule any out-of-home holiday activities, shopping, or appointments. Use this time however you see fit.

- Head into the holiday season with a positive attitude this year. Make the decision to be happy, joyous, loving, calm, and emotionally connected to all your friends and family throughout the season.
- December 25 will arrive whether you are ready for it or not, so trim down your to-do list to the bare essentials.
- Relieve holiday stress with the touch of your fingers by simply brushing them lightly back and forth along your inner forearm whenever you feel jittery or nervous. This soothing move causes levels of stress hormones to plummet, according to Miami's Touch Research Institute.
- Focus your mind and de-stress with floating candles! According to the centuries-old Chinese practice of feng shui, if you place a shallow bowl of floating tea lights next to your desk, you will induce calm and pump up your brainpower.
- Pour a mugful of steaming hot cocoa, curl up on the sofa, and watch *It's a Wonderful Life*.

FUN FACTS: CHRISTMAS

Using the abbreviation "Xmas" instead of "Christmas" dates back a long time. "Christ" in Greek is "Xristos," and "Xmas" was used as early as the fifteen hundreds.

- Throw another log into the fireplace and put on your favorite holiday CD.
- Take frequent deep-breathing breaks to cope with holiday-induced anxiety. Don't strive to create a perfect holiday; expect that families will fight, food will burn, presents won't fit. Have a good time anyway.
- Make it a point to compliment a stranger every day during the holiday season.
- Remember your milkman, sanitation worker, letter carrier, and newspaper boy or girl with a small holiday gift.
- Bring a decorated miniature Christmas tree to someone in a hospital or nursing home.
- Play fill-in-the-blank every day. Post a refrigerator note written on holiday stationary that says, "This holiday season I'm thankful for _____." Especially when things get hectic, it's important to stop just for a moment and keep things in perspective.
- Remember that peace on Earth starts with peace in our homes and in our hearts. Merry Christmas!

Grace Notes
for December . . .

Hanukkah

This eight-day festival of lights is a joyous Jewish
holiday celebrating the miraculous victory of the Jews
over the Syrians in the second century B.C.E. When the
Jews retook Jerusalem, they found their holiest of
temples in shambles. They cleaned and repaired it, then
observed an eight-day feast of rededication. According
to tradition, although there was only enough
consecrated oil to keep the light burning for one
night, miraculously the oil lasted for eight days.

Health

Feasting is such an important part of Hanukkah that rabbis
actually banned fasting during the holiday. Foods fried in
oil (latkes, or potato pancakes, and jelly doughnuts) are
popular . . . so remember to eat in moderation!

Fitness

Make it a point to get your workout done in the morning, so you can celebrate each evening of the holiday without guilt. Bring along fitness items while you travel during the holiday season. Pack sneakers, fitness clothes, fitness bands, hand weights, and even an exercise video to squeeze in some fitness during holiday travel.

HOME Décor

Create a display of menorahs—the one your grandmother brought with her from Poland, the one that you made as a child, the one your daughter created out of Popsicle sticks and birthday candles, the one your parents gave you as a wedding present. Nothing could be more beautiful or meaningful.

HOMEkeeping and Organization

Make your very own beeswax candles for the family menorah. Beeswax is sold in sheets in lots of different colors, and easy to make into candles. Simply place a length of wick onto a sheet, and then roll the sheet tightly around the wick. Press the edge of the wax sheet to the roll, and you've got a beautiful homemade candle.

Family

Play the dreidel game with your kids.

Self

Research Jewish cultural landmarks in your area. When in New York, make a point of visiting the Jewish Museum of Art, which originally opened in 1904 with just a small handful of donated pieces. Today it houses one of the world's largest collections of Jewish artwork and continues to support artists by commissioning new designs. Read a book or a novel about the women of the Old Testament. Anita Diamant's *The Red Tent* is a good one.

Kwanzaa

Kwanzaa is an African-American holiday that
celebrates family, community, and culture. Celebrated
from December 26 through January 1, the holiday has its
origins in the first harvest celebrations of Africa, from
which it takes its name. The name Kwanzaa comes from
the phrase "*matunda ya kwanza*" which means
"first fruits" in Swahili. Each night of candle lighting,
feasting, and reflection represents a different basic
principal from unity to faith. It is a cultural
but not a religious holiday, and can be
celebrated by people of all faiths.

Health

Kwanzaa is a harvest festival, and thus *mazao* (crops) are an
important part of the celebration. Be sure to make your
Kwanzaa feast heavy on fruits and vegetables. Look through
your cookbooks for African recipes for vegetarian stews.

Fitness

On the first night of Kwanzaa, make a traditional vow to improve your health by continuing your regular fitness routine.

Home

Display a Kinara (candleholder) holding seven candles (three green, three red, and a black candle in the center). Honor your ancestors by prominently displaying old family photographs this week.

Family

Create a Kwanzaa place mat (called a *mkeka*) for each family member. Weave strips of colored paper together in green, black, and red (the colors of the Kwanzaa flag).

Self

Take a moment to see how the basic principles of Kwanzaa figure into your own life and the communities of which you are a part: *Umoja* (unity), *Kujichagulia* (self-determination), *Ujima* (collective work and responsibility), *Ujamaa* (cooperative economics), *Nia* (purpose), *Kuumba* (creativity), and *Imani* (faith).

New Year's Eve

An evening of anticipation and celebration
for the arrival of the New Year. A time to
reflect upon the past and begin anew.

Health

Follow a Cuban tradition and eat twelve grapes at the stroke
of midnight. The twelve grapes signify the last twelve
months of the year. Unlike champagne, grapes won't give
you a headache.

Fitness

Sign up for a community-sponsored New Year's Eve 5K walk
or run.

Home

Spread the joy! Sprinkle sparkly confetti on all your tables today, from the breakfast table to the dinner buffet table. And have your entire family use long-stemmed glasses all day today . . . from the orange juice and milk to your champagne.

Family

Try this great soul-cleansing ritual from professional organizer Ana Popielnicki of Options by Ana in Somers, Connecticut: Have everyone write down any worries, problems, bitter feelings, unhappy memories, or sad times from the past twelve months, seal them all in an envelope, and burn them on New Year's Eve.

Self

In addition to your New Year's finery, be sure to wear a few treasured reminders of the things—and people—most important to you. Your mother's pearls, a grandmother's shawl, the macaroni bracelet your daughter made in art class. New Year's Eve is a time to honor memories as well.

The authors would love to hear from you. Please log onto
SimpleStepsProgram.com
for information about Simple Steps, and feel
free to e-mail any questions or comments to
SimpleStepsProgram@hotmail.com

The authors are available for lectures and workshops.
Details will be sent upon request.
SIMPLE STEPS
c/o Reflections Lifestyle Workshops
P.O. Box 128, Guilford, CT 06437

Lisa Lelas (left) is the owner of Life Styling Professional Organizing of Guilford, Connecticut. She is a personal life coach, a columnist, and a motivational speaker on the subject of organizing and life mapping (www.LifeStylingwithLisa.com). **Linda McClintock** (center) is now a certified feng shui consultant (www.crystalreflections.com), and **Beverly Zingarella** (right) is a stay-at-home mother of three children. Collectively known as the "Guilford Girls" (after their home town in Connecticut), they have appeared on *Oprah*, *Today*, and NBC news.